Promises, Promises

Breaking Faith
in Canadian Politics

—◄○►—

Anthony Hyde

VIKING

VIKING
Published by the Penguin Group
Penguin Books Canada Ltd, 10 Alcorn Avenue, Toronto, Ontario, Canada
M4V 3B2
Penguin Books Ltd, 27 Wrights Lane, London W8 5TZ, England
Penguin Books USA Inc., 375 Hudson Street, New York, New York 10014,
U.S.A.
Penguin Books Australia Ltd, Ringwood, Victoria, Australia
Penguin Books (NZ) Ltd, cnr Rosedale and Airborne Roads, Albany, Auckland
1310, New Zealand

Penguin Books Ltd, Registered Offices: Harmondsworth, Middlesex, England

First published 1997
10 9 8 7 6 5 4 3 2 1

Copyright © Tusitala Inc., 1997

Printed and bound in Canada on acid-free paper ∞

Canadian Cataloguing in Publication Data

Hyde, Anthony, 1946–
    Promises, Promises

ISBN 0-670-87710-7

1. Canada – Politics and government – 1963–1984.* 2. Canada – Politics and
government – 1984–1993.* 3. Canada Politics and government – 1984– .*
4. Electioneering – Canada. 5. Political parties – Canada – Platforms. I. Title.

FC635.H92 1997   324.271'013   C97-930457-1
F1034.2.H92 1997

Visit Penguin Canada's web site at **www.penguin.ca**

for
Barbara Bambridge
who first read to me pages from Canada's story

Acknowledgments

This is a book of political opinions, and of course the people noted below do not necessarily, or even probably, share those opinions—which makes the help they offered me all the more generous. So I'd like to thank Val Sears, for his wonderful memories; Duncan Cameron, who steered me toward the Vets, and Mac Johnston at the *Legion Magazine*; Denise Doherty-Delorme, at the Canadian Federation of Students; Andrew Wernick, for reminding me of the importance of the hinterland; Mike Whittington, at Carleton, who's the co-author of a first-rate textbook, and gave me some excellent pointers; George Roseme, always full of astonishing insights, especially about American politics; Marianne Bluger Neily, who argued about the Bible; Heather Jon Maroney, who poked and prodded at various of my notions; and Henry Tarvainen, for his vigilant eye.

I'd also especially like to thank Jackie Kaiser and Cynthia Good, editors at Penguin, for giving me the opportunity to write the book, and who offered a good deal of help along the way. Richard Garner, as usual, heard all this first, and helped me think it through. Last, but definitely not least, I want to thank Kathleen Moses—her research assistance and editorial advice were crucial in the face of a tight deadline.

Now a promise made is a debt unpaid, and the trail has its own stern code . . .

    —Robert W. Service, *The Cremation of Sam McGee*

Contents

Preface

—◄o►—

Rant, Rant, Rant

I hate the GST, you hate the GST, *everybody* hates the GST.

If you run a small business, you hate the pernickety accounting it forces you to do, you hate the forms, and every time you deal with the GST's clumsy and aggressive bureaucracy, you end up furious.

But it's not just businessmen; no one, however innocent, escapes.

Schoolchildren buying their exercise books pay this tax; a woman who needs a new pair of winter boots pays it; and a man who stands in line for twenty minutes at Canadian Tire to buy what he needs to fix the kitchen sink, he pays it too . . . in fact everyone contributes to the limo and driver that take Paul Martin to work every morning, everyone chips in to pay all those bureaucrats to shuffle all that paper back and forth, day after day.

Except for food, every single purchase we make—from the most basic and necessary to the most frivolous—bears this tax. Shopping, as a small personal pleasure, now leaves a bad taste in the mouth; how can you buy yourself a treat when 7 per cent of your money goes to the Feds? Omnipresent and omnivorous, few taxes are more oppressive. They've always taxed the money we make—now they tax the money we spend. Totalitarianism, no doubt, is a political policeman's knock on the door at three in the morning; but it's also a government so voracious that it can't even leave you alone to buy a new pair of socks.

Naturally—*of course*—we owe all this to Brian Mulroney. Indeed, the GST must be counted as one of the major "achievements" of his government. And since the tax was almost universally abominated from the moment it was introduced—January 1, 1991—it became a principal issue in the 1993 election campaign and was central to the Conservative defeat. Actually, given the incompetence of Mr. Mulroney's government, given its corruption, given the notorious personalities associated with it—Lucien Bouchard, we should remember, was Brian Mulroney's personal creation—attacking the GST was almost excessive, *de trop*. But excess, God knows, has never troubled the Liberal Party of Canada. And so, day after day during that election, in speech after speech and thousands of television advertisements, Liberals high and low hammered away at the GST: they swore, pledged, *promised* to abolish it. They never let up. And it worked. The Liberals won. Jean Chrétien became Canada's new prime minister. And as soon as his government was sworn in . . . But everyone knows the story from that point on. The Liberals didn't do a thing about the GST. Replace it? They didn't even change its name.

And people grew angry—very, very angry.

Extraordinarily, even Liberals were angry. A few, like John Nunziata, became so angry that they were thrown out of the Liberal caucus. Sheila Copps, elevated to the cabinet but trapped by her virulent attacks on the tax—and her own promise to abolish it—actually resigned her seat and ran in a by-election, a dubious testament to parliamentary "honour."

But it didn't make any difference; anger at the Liberals' breach of promise was as pervasive as the tax itself. From Corner Brook to Kelowna, in cafés, bars and cafeterias, people grew more and more furious. Finally, on December 10, 1996, this extraordinary wave of anger crested and broke during a CBC "town hall" meeting. A waitress from Montreal, livid with rage, denounced the prime minister for breaking his promise to get rid of the GST, and he responded by grotesquely claiming that her question had been planted by the media. *That* only made the country angrier still, and within weeks the prime minister had fled the country for Asia.

Everyone is familiar with this saga—but what did it really mean? What was going on? Why were people so angry—what were the roots of this vast, bottomless, unappeasable rage?

Some people, of course, will find the answer to these questions so obvious that they won't even trouble to ask them. But I want to—because I think the real explanation is more important, and subtle, than it seems at first glance.

To understand what I mean, consider the tax itself.

Yes, it's oppressive. But the whole tax regime in Canada can be described that way. Endlessly rising rates of income tax have turned tax avoidance into a major industry; sales and excise taxes, especially on cigarettes and liquor, have created a huge "black" economy; and payroll taxes have made the hiring of new employees the solution of last resort for any reasonable business enterprise. The GST is certainly part of this system, but it's only one part—why, then, has it become the focus of such universal anger and disdain? And although the GST was undoubtedly poorly administered in the beginning, it's equally true that things have become a good deal better. Besides, let's keep a sense of proportion. Every civilized industrial country—every country which uses its tax revenue to provide citizens with decent, dignified pensions, reasonable access to education and universal health care—has some form of value-added tax similar to the GST. The Brits pay it, the French pay it, the Germans pay it, *even the Italians pay it*; and of course they don't like it, but the irritation they feel is nothing like the anger we've seen in Canada. By any reasonable measure, Canadian anger against the GST is out of all proportion to the tax itself.

But of course there's another element here, and an important one.

The Liberals *lied* about the GST.

Jean Chrétien *lied* about the GST.

And there must be no mistake about this—they did lie. The Liberal Party has never lacked for lawyers, but no amount of legal or semantic quibbling can hide the truth—the Liberals, and Jean Chrétien, lied. But … *so what*? Maybe I'm cynical. After all, I have to confess that I was born and raised in Ottawa, and have lived most of my life within a few hundred yards of Parliament Hill. So I have few illusions about our national politicians—I mean, I see these people in bars. But surely no Canadian with an IQ over 50 actually expects politicians to tell the truth. On the contrary: most of us assume that all politicians are liars. Jean Chrétien, in point of fact, isn't even especially untruthful. And all that distinguishes the Liberals, when it comes to lying, is that they can do it in both our national languages. Perhaps—to be completely honest myself—I should even confess a bit more. Like everyone else, I find the GST exceedingly annoying, but it never occurred to me, for a single second, that the Liberals were going to repeal it. The tax makes far too much money—and Paul Martin, after all, *likes* that limo to pick him up every morning. Moreover, I don't really think most Canadians expected them to abolish it either, not when they considered things *rationally*.

But that's the point. Anger—the response of so many Canadians to *l'affaire GST*—is an emotional response, not a rational one. Which is fair enough—because the Liberals' assault on the GST wasn't rational in the first place. It was purely emotional. They didn't *argue* against the tax, they never *reasonably* set out any *rational* alternative to it. They simply *promised* to repeal it.

They *promised*.

But promises, including political promises, are special—and that's what this book is about.

Chapter One

—◄o►—

What's in a Promise?

*T*he part of Ottawa where I grew up is called New Edinburgh, and includes Sussex Drive where the prime minister lives. Along here, the Rideau River flows into the Ottawa, over the Rideau Falls, whose "curtain" of water—*le rideau*—suggested to Champlain the river's name. All summer, as children, we played beside the riverbank, in the fall we played football in the parks, and one of our boyish tests of courage was to walk *behind* the falls—behind the curtain—which was, in fact, fairly easily done, for there were caves and grottoes, recesses, in the rock. Of course my mother, God bless her, never knew about *that.* Her particular fear came in the winter, with freeze-up. Each year, the Rideau freezes over, and the ice is no doubt thick enough to support a tank, but my mother would live with the anxiety that I might try to cross over, slip through a crevasse, and be swept away. So, each year, there was an early winter ritual: my brother and I would be compelled to *promise*—on pain of God knows what damnation from my mother's Toronto-born, C.G.I.T.* heart— never, *never,* to go out on the Rideau River ice. And I promised. And guess what?—I never did.

* For the benefit of younger ladies, C.G.I.T. stands for *Canadian Girls in Training.* It was (may still be, for all I know) a United Church equivalent to the Girl Guides, which was identified with the Anglicans. Its aim was to produce *good* girls, in a purely Protestant meaning of the word.

Promises are like that.

Promises, in the first place, are always personal. I can make a

promise *to* you—but I can't make one *for* you. Promises are
always our own. And promises are always absolute. My mother
wanted me to promise, because that was the ultimate test, the
absolute guarantee. For my part, having given her my promise,
what more could I say? Once you've said, *that's a promise*, there's
nothing to add. When we make a promise, we always put ourselves—the meaning of our character—on the line.

But promises are never *just* personal.

According to the dictionary, a promise is "an oral or written
agreement to do, or not to do, something,"[1]—and so, in effect,
all promises are *contracts*. Indeed, the most elementary form of
obligation between two parties is the promissory note, "an unconditional written *promise* to pay a certain sum of money at a
definite time."[2] Contracts of this sort must be ancient, going
back to an epoch when the law was uncertain, and personal reputation and community standing—even if the community lived
in a cave—were the best security you could have. Business was
done face to face; a man's word had to be his bond—if you
broke it, you got down to six-guns, shoot-outs and endless
feuds.

So the idea of *promise*, though often surrounded with a sentimental glow (*Promises* has been used as a title by most of the
romantic novelists from Catherine Gaskin to Belva Plain),
actually has a harder, tougher core of meaning. Promises don't
simply hold two people together, they hold the world together
as well; as a *general rule*, promises must be kept, otherwise they
become meaningless, and so everyone has a stake in every
promise, even those we don't make ourselves. Society notes this

in a variety of ways. For example, even the simplest arrangements have traditionally been marked with a handshake or a drink, little ceremonies that make all promises *solemn*:

> I promise to do my best,
> To be true to myself, my God and Canada;
> I will help others and accept the Guiding Law.

From the Guide Promise to the vows of marriage, promises are surrounded by ritual and symbolism; when we make promises, we often put on special clothes, play special music, go to special places. All this underlines the gravity of promises and expresses the intensity of feeling associated with them. To the same end, promises are often made in front of *witnesses*—peers, family members, a religious congregation. These witnesses are always important, a social extension of individual responsibility and conscience—and even when they're deliberately excluded, in *secret* promises, they play their part. Witnesses, like ceremony, add weight to promise making. But this functions only within certain limits. Witnesses sanction promises, but they certainly can't force the person making a promise to keep it. Don't worry; if you break your marriage vows, all those people who watched you make them in church aren't going to come around and beat you up. All they can do, as you stand there, is serve as a reminder that your name and reputation are at stake, and, further, testify to the general importance of promises in the larger community. *We're here because all promises are important, yours especially so.* Naturally, the more important a promise is, the more impressive the witnesses invoked to sanction it. And the most important witness, of course, is God. Vows, oaths, pledges, covenants—whole categories of promises are made with God, or in His Sight. He's the ultimate witness. So, when we become witnesses ourselves—and promise to tell the truth—we hold His Book in our hand.

And so we come to the Bible—hardly surprising. Since promises can't be enforced, we have no choice except to *trust* people who make us promises; we must take them on *faith*—and faith very much defines the meaning of promise. Just as promises begin with our most intense feelings and commitments, but are then woven through the whole fabric of our social relations, so our deepest beliefs and ethical conceptions are woven into our ideas of promise making and keeping.

"Promise," in fact, is one of the most important words in the Bible—Christianity *is* "the promise of life which is in Christ."[3] But before we get to Christ, we have to deal with the *covenant*, which is simply *promise* wearing a clerical collar or a yarmulke— "the promise made by God to man, as recorded in the Bible."[4]

That record, however, is a complex one, more so than we normally assume. The very first covenant is actually between God and Noah and "every living creature," with God promising to save Noah from the flood and then instituting the rainbow as a perpetual "token" of their bond. The arrangement is virtually one-sided; Noah, though he's clearly acknowledging God, really promises nothing in return. And the same is true when God first appears to Abraham. Initially, God's covenant with the Patriarch is an unconditional promise of land—all the land between the Nile and the Euphrates—and there's nothing that Abraham is required to do for it. Only much later, intervening in Abraham's rather complicated sex life, does the Lord appear once more, this time to establish a covenant—a further promise of land, and numerous progeny—which finally makes a specific demand upon him: Abraham, and his whole male line, would be circumcised—"it shall be a token of the covenant betwixt me and you."[5] As a "token" this may seem peculiar, even bizarre, but it must be remembered that circumcision was originally symbolic; relatively little flesh was cut away, at least in comparison with the total mutilation that later became common practice.[6] It was a "sign" or "seal" indicating acceptance of the agreement.

These developments, taken together, establish the first stage of the Biblical covenant. At this point, it seems a rather odd bargain; although we're apparently operating in the spiritual realm, it's almost wholly materialistic. Of course, Abraham is accepting God *as* God, but that isn't really stressed, and the substance of the agreement concerns real estate, political power and—weirdly—the foreskins of infant boys. But this original bargain, although never denied, now undergoes significant modification. Much time passes. Abraham has long since gone to his rest. His descendants, taken into captivity by the Egyptian pharaoh, have endured years of servitude, but have finally escaped and under the extraordinary leadership of Moses are attempting to regain their ancestral homeland. This effort is fraught with difficulty and dissension, and eventually both Moses and his God are questioned. In this crisis, God appears again, and on Mount Sinai renews his covenant. Commanding Moses to fashion two stone tablets, He then says: "Write thou these words: for after the tenor of these words I have made a covenant with thee and with Israel ... And he wrote upon the tablets *the words of the covenant, the ten commandments.*"[7]

With this, the whole emphasis of the covenant shifts. The bargain is no longer so one-sided: God's adherents will now obey God's *law*—not only His commandments, but a whole host of prescriptions about social behaviour and diet. Although there's still a good deal in the covenant about land and political power, its definition is much more intellectual and spiritual—significantly, the covenant is now embodied in *words*. Finally, the mark of the covenant's acceptance changes. The peculiar hostility toward boys' foreskins persists, but the token of the covenant with Moses is to be the sabbath, strictly observed, and applying to the entire community: "Verily my sabbaths ye shall keep: for it is a sign between me and you throughout your generations; that ye may know that I am the LORD that doth sanctify you . . . the children of Israel shall keep the sabbath, to observe the sabbath throughout their generations, for a perpetual covenant."[8]

Here we have the covenant as it came down to Christians. And we must remember that it was vitally important to them. Jesus was a Jew. The first Christians were Jews. One of the earliest tasks of Christianity was finding a definition for itself apart from Judaism. And it's worth noting, by the way, that the word "testament"—as in Old and New Testament—would be more correctly translated as "covenant." That's what Christianity is— a *new* covenant. Christians believed that the coming of Christ caused the old patriarchal and Mosaic covenant to be superseded, and saw it as being both fulfilled and incorporated into a new "promise" of Christ.

But in what way was the covenant—God's promise—changed?

The *locus classicus* for this discussion is Paul's letter to the Galatians, probably the earliest surviving Christian text.[9] Who were the Galatians? God, presumably, knows—academics, of course, argue ceaselessly about it. But they were likely ethnic Gauls, living in central Asia Minor or in the Roman province of Galatia. They had been Christianized, but were now relapsing into Judaism; they were questioning the legitimacy of Paul's ministry, defining true religion in terms of adherence to the Mosaic law, and insisting upon circumcision as a mark of that adherence.

Paul's rebuttal of their position stands as a crucial statement of the differences between the old covenant and the new. Now, Paul insists, everything depends on *faith*. Paul readily concedes that before his conversion he was a keen adherent of the Mosaic law, that he was "exceedingly zealous of the traditions of my fathers." But his new gospel is a direct expression of faith, and this faith—not the law—truly defines the relationship between God and Man. "This only would I learn of you," he asks, "Received ye the Spirit by the works of the law, or by the hearing of faith? . . . He therefore that ministereth to you the Spirit, and worketh miracles among you, doeth he it by the works of the law, or by the hearing of faith?" The heirs of the original covenant, he declares, are not defined by their acceptance of the law, but by their acceptance of Christ, through faith. "Know ye therefore that they which are of the faith, the same are the children of Abraham." The *law* has been superseded. In fact, "Christ hath redeemed us from the curse of the law . . . that we might receive *the promise of the Spirit through faith*." If we have faith, we are the true heirs of Abraham, for "to Abraham and his seed were the promises made" and "if the inheritance be of the law, it is no more of promise: but God gave it to Abraham by promise. Wherefore then serveth the law?" The law, Paul believes, was a stopgap, a temporary measure, "till the seed

9

should come to whom the promise was made . . . that the promise by faith of Jesus Christ might be given to them that believe."

Faith, belief, promise—these are the ties that now bind Man and God together, that form the new covenant rather than the old law. As for men's foreskins, they are no longer of spiritual significance: "For in Jesus Christ neither circumcision availeth any thing, nor uncircumcision; but faith which worketh by love." Under Christ, Paul declares, "the law is fulfilled in one word, even in this; Thou shalt love thy neighbour as thyself." But this, of course, is not law in the older, Mosaic sense, but a reminder that, having faith in Jesus Christ, we must live it. If we do, we shall be "*the children of promise.*"[10]†

Inevitably, this all seems somewhat esoteric, but the importance of this redefined covenant for our feeling and thinking about *promise* should be clear enough. Promise emerges from our deepest spiritual selves, and is intimately bound up with faith and belief. Most important of all, *promise is greater than the law.* Of course, promise is always marked by the law; implicitly, all promises are contracts. But this is only notionally true; it would even be possible to argue that, in Christian terms, God's grace operates as a kind of *force majeure*, annulling all other arrangements. And even if most people expect that their faith will be rewarded, there's clearly no way we can hold God to account, and most Christians would see any "failure" on God's part as constituting a proof that their own faith—their part of the bargain—was defective. This is a subtle point, however. Just because promises involve our faith, we effectively judge them by

† I have put all references in the preceding paragraph into this citation.

a higher standard than the law provides. God is absolutely trust-worthy, *and we judge anyone to whom we give our faith by that standard.* Legalistic quibbling about promises is immediately sensed as betrayal. When we accept a promise from someone, we give them our trust, our faith, and we have no recourse—because, by accepting a promise, we're saying that no recourse is possible or legitimate anyway.

Promises work by faith, and are beyond the law—the Bible adds this crucial dimension to our understanding of promise. But religious feeling touches promise in other ways as well, and we can see that by tracing a little run of logic whose premises are part of what Paul was talking about.

First, think about the gulf between God and Man. Although there is no logical reason why promises can't be made between equals—and many are—our feelings about promising are con-ditioned by the assumption of a considerable gulf between the two parties; in the case of our relations with God, of course, that gulf couldn't be greater. What happens, when we extend a promise, is that we bridge that gulf, whether it's defined in terms of power, or wealth, or simply distance: "I promise to come home to you."

But there are some important corollaries to this. When pow-erful figures extend promises, they are effectively constraining their power; and when weaker figures accept promises, they are, interestingly, exercising power. We can even see this in relation to God. "The promise of Christ" is the promise of salvation, of redemption, of eternal life. It's extended to us by an omnipotent God—but, by accepting it, we gain a certain access to His omnipotence. We too become powerful. We too will live eternally, in Heaven. In effect, we are guaranteeing our future. This *future reference* of promise is, of course, part of its basic definition, and we use it in ordinary language when we say "it promises to be a fair day" or "he's a young man of promise."

Bearing these two points in mind—promise as an exercising of power and always in reference to the future—we encounter an even more basic layer of meaning, more primitive than the religious. Promising—the rites, rituals and ceremonies connected to it—is literally magical. This seems startling, especially in connection to politics, but then words like "charisma" and "spellbinding" aren't part of our political vocabulary for nothing. Magic, as defined by Bronislaw Malinowski, is "a practical art consisting of acts which are only a means to a definite end expected to follow later on."[11] Promises work in much the same way. Like magic, promises allow us to control future events, or at least give us the illusion that we do. Like magic, promises are usually enacted in a context of rite and ritual, and are surrounded with emotional intensity—enhanced by music, costume, sacred words and so on. They rely on faith and belief, not rationality, for their effect. We don't judge promises rationally, or not wholly rationally. When someone makes a promise, we may try to make a rational judgment as to whether the promise *can* be kept, but that judgment is profoundly influenced, and often completely overcome, by our subjective, emotional hope that it will be. This emotional, subjective side is developed even further in our relationship to the person making the promise. Any rational judgments we may make about such figures are inextricably bound up with our *feelings* about them. Since personal frailties—which might be the basis for rational judgment—can get in the way of belief, individuals who are involved in magical ceremonies are usually masked or costumed, and given enhanced social status, so they will become somewhat removed from rational contemplation altogether, turned into *figures*, shamans or priests. Finally, all of these judgments and feelings are themselves subservient to the *wish*, an almost wholly emotional element, which the promise embodies—that crops will come up, or the GST will be cancelled. Promises, then, are believed to the degree that we have confidence or faith in the promise-giver, and when the promise touches some deeper wish within us. We want to get well, we believe in our doctor, we have faith in the power of modern medicine—so a pill, even if it's a placebo, can cure us. Ultimately, this system is circular and self-validating, but all the more powerful for it: it profoundly supports our belief in belief. Accordingly, when we utter the words "*I promise,*" we cast a spell; when we accept a promise, we fall under it. This is one of the reasons why quite outrageous promises can find acceptance. Often enough, the power of the faith elicited by a promise can overcome rational objections to its contents. Indeed, we often believe and accept promises precisely because we wish to avoid a rational contemplation of the issue a promise raises. We know we're going to die, but we don't want to die; hence, despite the lack of any rationally acceptable evidence for it, the promise of everlasting life becomes very "believable." In the same way, we know the deficit is a major economic problem. And so the promise of "supply-side" economics—that we can eliminate the deficit by first expanding it through lower taxes—falls on fertile ground. George Bush, in attacking Ronald Reagan's "voodoo economics," was more correct than he knew. "The function of magic," as Malinowski says, "is to ritualize man's optimism, to enhance his faith in the victory of hope over fear."[12] Do that on television, and you can

be repeatedly elected to high office—as Mr. Reagan's career so abundantly proved.

Promises, working by faith and operating above the law, allow us to bridge even the widest gulfs between people, and by giving us control over the future invest us with magical power. But our feelings about *promise* are not only formed by our relationship with the Almighty. Anyone who looks into *promise* quickly discovers that, yes, we make our most important promises with God —but we make some pretty important promises to *children,* too.

With children, all the principles of promising we've seen so far still operate, but the roles are reversed. We, as parents, take the place of God. Children *have faith* in us. Children trust us. Children look up to us. Arguably, since parents play a crucial *material* role in the lives of children, the gulf between parents and children is even greater than that between God and Man. If God forsakes us, we may lose a future life; if our parents fail us, we perish now. Promises bridge this extraordinary gap of total dependency. And obviously children can't hold parents to their promises—any more than we can hold God to account—but most parents, when it comes to promising, feel accountable to something greater than any law. The same is true going the other way. Extracting promises from children is a way of imposing a very special obligation on them. Think of my mother and myself. Or, to take a rather different example, we actually have Norman Mailer demanding of "his eighteen-year-old daughter, a Freshman now at Barnard, that she not take marijuana, and never LSD, until she had completed her education, *a mean promise to extract in these apocalyptic times.*"[13]

But the relationship of promising to children, even though it generally conforms to what we know about promises, adds to and emphasizes the idea in special ways.

Although we talk about "developing faith" in a religious sense, this process of learning and acceptance is given a special twist in relation to children. Trusting us to keep our promises, their trust is reinforced when we do: and so the confidence they develop in us becomes part of becoming confident in general. The world, in a certain sense, becomes a series of promises *kept*. Children, through promises, also learn to trust themselves. Keeping their own promises—to parents—is one of the ways children learn a sense of responsibility. Keeping promises to their peers, even in opposition to their parents—*promise not to tell*—is a crucial act of self-definition. So promises help children define what's important, and define them *as* important.

All this is reinforced because promises, on the one hand, are connected to children's deepest *wishes*, and, on the other, to their most profound *anxieties*. Around Christmas and birthdays and summer holidays, children *want* and *hope for* and we promise to satisfy those wants, fulfil those hopes. And of course there's a definite materialistic side to this; wishes, if not quite defining greed, often seem to work out to have a monetary value, and though my CCM skates (to take you back in time) weren't worth all the land between the Nile and the Euphrates, they were still worth a lot to me. The gifts and emoluments of childhood—so often what we promise—add up to love, but they also establish an economic side to promise (a contract, remember) which it never quite escapes.

But promises, in a sense, are not always positive. Promises can be threats, invoking fear—*Now promise to be good!*—and parents often use promises this way. Sometimes, this is a simple promise of retribution, punishment for bad behaviour. More often, it's a technique of intimidation, a kind of warning. We want children *not* to do something, so we remind them, emphatically, of the negative consequences if they do—including parental displeasure, the most important negative of them all. But just because we do use a promise, which is so bound up with trust and faith, we're trying to communicate to the child that the behaviour we want is ultimately rooted in a concern for their safety and well-being; the promise acts as a special emphasis; and of course children are experts at picking up such signals. But we also use promises, in a different way, to help children overcome their fear. We promise *to come back* for children, when they're afraid of being abandoned—at nursery school or summer camp; we promise children that they'll *get better,* when they're sick. Because children trust us, our promises are reassuring. And because, sometimes, parents want reassurance, they seek promises from their kids—as Norman Mailer did.

There's a fine children's book which illustrates this very well—*A Promise Is a Promise,* by Robert Munsch, Michael Kusugak and Vladyana Krykorka.[14] It's a story I can identify with, since it's also about kids disappearing through the ice. Here, though, we're dealing with *serious* ice, up in the Northwest Territories. An Inuit mother, as anxious as my own, tells her children that a race of trolls, the Quallupilliut, live under the sea ice and grab children who venture onto it without their parents. So if you want to fish, she tells her daughter, Allashua, go on the lake, where the ice is much thicker and safer. The young lady agrees:

"I promise to go fishing in the lake and not in the ocean," she says, "and a promise is a promise."

But Inuit girls can be naughty, and of course Allashua breaks her promise, goes out on the ice, and is dragged under by the Quallupilliut. Desperately, as she sinks, she calls out that if the trolls let her go, she'll bring all her brothers and sisters out on the ice for them to catch. The trolls, agreeing, throw her back, and Allashua crawls wretchedly home, where her parents comfort her. But what are they to do? As her family reminds her, "a promise is a promise." Mother, of course, has the answer. She invites the Quallupilliut into the house, ostensibly while she says goodbye to her (fairly considerable) brood. She gives each of the kids some bread, saying to the trolls, "This is not for you." But the trolls want some, and when the mother gives them each a slice, they love it. And when the mother gives her children some candy, the same thing happens again. Then the father starts to dance, telling the trolls that dancing isn't for them, either. But they want to try; and when they do, they love it as well. And then the mother starts dancing . . . which is the signal for the children to creep out of the house, down to the ice, just as Allashua had promised. But the trolls are so happy dancing that they don't notice what's happened, and when Allashua calls out that here they are, all the children, just as she'd *promised,* they don't hear. Only after Allashua has taken her brothers and sisters safely back to shore, do the Quallupilliut realize they've been tricked. They're furious, but as Allashua reminds them, "A promise is what you were given and a promise is what you got. I brought my brothers and sisters to the sea ice. But you were not here. A promise is a promise."

As a former minister of Indian Affairs and Northern Development, one might have expected Jean Chrétien to absorb some of this aboriginal wisdom when it comes to promises—and how to get out of them—but presumably he was too busy with his briefing books. If he'd been paying attention, he would have learned how deeply *promise* is imbedded in childhood—as warning, as reassurance and as a touchstone of personal responsibility regardless of the consequences.

But *promise* goes even deeper than this.

To understand the real bedrock of promise, we have to understand that all the individual promises—the promises of gifts, the promises that are warnings, the reassurances, the prayers, the vows, the pledges—create a whole which is much greater than the sum of its parts. The promise we feel for ourselves from Christ, all the promises we make to children, create a great, global commitment, an implicit universal promise: *I promise to look after you, I promise that everything will be all right.*

Robert Penn Warren, in one of his finest poems, returns to his childhood home, resurrects in memory the figures of his parents, and wonders about the meaning of their lives and their deaths. In the last line, they answer, *We died only that every promise might be fulfilled.*[15] Exactly. Every particular promise creates some single future—my own little future, or Allashua's—but the greater promise is of the future itself, a future that stretches even into Eternity. This is the "big promise" that lies behind all the little promises, and it bears repeating: *I promise to look after you, I promise that everything will be all right.* Created and reinforced in childhood, this "big promise" is the foundation for all our promises—it supports the faith we call upon when we make a promise, and the faith that we extend when we believe in one: and the breach of any particular promise breaks this greater promise too. *Promise*, therefore, becomes a complex system of interconnected elements, working from the particular to the general, and back again. Promises only work, in general, to the extent that everybody keeps them in the particular, and when we lose faith in "the big promise" all the little ones are cast in doubt. The *fragility* of such a system is obvious, but its strength is even greater. It's universal and ubiquitous, shared by everyone and working in most aspects of life. And it both harnesses and expresses some of the most powerful human emotions.

Can we summarize?

Promises are always contracts, often between very unequal parties—promises usually bridge a *gulf.*

Promises are sanctioned by the community, *witnesses*, ritualized social practice—but they are nonetheless beyond the *law.*

Promises, finally, rest on *faith*—a faith rooted in childhood and defining our deepest self.

A promise is a promise, said Allashua, and clearly didn't quite understand what she meant—or that she meant so much. Most people don't. Bridging the gulf between God and Man, weaving ties of love and hope and reassurance between parents and their children, promises are special and extraordinarily powerful. Is it any wonder that they are perilous as well?

Just ask Mr. Chrétien.

Chapter Two

—◄o►—

Talking Politics

*P*olitical promises are part of our political discourse . . . which is a fancy way of saying *how we talk about politics.*

And we do talk about politics in a particular way—political talk has its own vocabulary, grammar and style.

To a degree, this is established by the politicians themselves, the way *they* talk . . . which, in Canada, is largely a matter of evasion and circumlocution, a desperate but usually successful search to find the most long-winded way of saying as little as possible. Our politicians are second to none at this. Mr. Chrétien, surely, has an inimitable line in the bewildering. Going back in time, John Diefenbaker's extraordinary, meandering sentences—in which he could change the subject three times within a single clause—were deliberate exercises in obfuscation. If he started a sentence and didn't like where it was heading—or so he once told a reporter—"I change direction or don't finish the sentence. That way, they can't pin me down."[1] Mr. Diefenbaker's principal opponent, Lester Pearson, took a different tack. A product of the civil service, his perorations always had the quality of memos written by a bureaucrat determined to cover his nether parts, and no one could ever remember what he'd said because the audience was usually asleep halfway through his dissertation. More positively—and recalling Mr. Diefenbaker again—his standard salutation, *My fellow Canadians*, made an immediate connection to his audience, and summed up, in a phrase, his particular brand of populism. And, equally effective in a different way, was Pierre Trudeau's steely look into the camera and then that slightly ominous, *Friends*. (In regard to Mr. Pearson, I asked Val Sears, a journalistic veteran of that period, how LBP normally began a speech; after thinking a moment, Mr. Sears replied, "I can't remember.")

But the verbal behaviour of politicians at any particular time is only an overlay on a well-established pattern of political discourse, which has come down to us, apparently, from time immemorial. Since he has a particular importance in this history, I'll stay with John Diefenbaker; here's a sample from Peter Newman's book about him, *Renegade in Power* (still one of the finest pieces of Canadian political journalism):

> Although Diefenbaker made a great many specific *promises* during his cross-country electioneering *junkets*, his *platform* did not add up to a co-ordinated plan for the grand design he was touting for Canada. Its strongest and most precise *planks* dealt with parliamentary reform. He *pledged* himself . . .[2]

Platforms and planks and pledges . . . it's a language we're all familiar with. If Mr. Martin brings down a tough budget, we are asked to *tighten our belts*; if Ms. Copps, God forbid, were to incur Mr. Chrétien's displeasure, she would be *taken out to the woodshed*, there to suffer scarcely imaginable chastisements. Politics, as defined by this language, becomes a series of town hall meetings and political debates conducted during fall fairs, the candidates getting up on their *soapboxes*—more of those platforms and planks—and hecklers merrily hooting in the crowd.

Of course, this world is purely mythological; no one, with the possible exception of Preston Manning and the people who design Christmas cards, actually believes that it ever existed. But, like all myths, it *pretends* to be merely an anachronism; long, long ago, we're asked to believe, there actually was a Canada in which apple pies cooled on kitchen window sills, and Mr. Bouchard's happy *habitants* sang folk songs and wove pure wool along the verdant banks of the Saguenay. *Promise* is part of this, drenched in the same nostalgia. Indeed, given its peculiar associations with childhood, it's an especially important element in such constructions. Thus, in a series of advertisements for mbanx (an effusion of the Bank of Montreal) we see a young girl, apparently aboriginal, thoughtfully surveying a carefully arranged "natural" landscape; she muses aloud, "Wouldn't it be nice if people kept their promises?" But whether it's this young lady, or Mr. Christie baking his cookies, such images only exist to help large corporations, financial, political or otherwise, peddle their wares. There never was a time or a world like that.

Or was there?

The myth is trying to connect, however vaguely, with a sentimentally imagined rural and small-town world, sometime in the nineteenth century, or perhaps early in the twentieth—the world of *kitsch;* but the real Canada of that time had little to do with such notions; and so far as the history of *promise*, and its particular role in our political discourse, is concerned, the situation was rather more complicated.

In fact, in the years after Confederation, there were no political promises in the modern sense, for two very good reasons. First, there were no political parties in the modern sense— and second, we didn't even have national elections, not as we know them today. Elections were held over months, almost province by province; candidates would run as individuals, and only declare their "party" loyalty after they were confident as to who would form the government. It wasn't until 1878 that we had simultaneous national elections in the east, and it wasn't until 1893, when Wilfrid Laurier whipped the Liberals into shape, that anything like our modern party system began to function. Up to that point, "individuals were recruited and supported in elections to the House of Commons by local elites and were more responsive to them than to the national party leadership."[3]

The effect of this on political promises is obvious; you can't have political promises without a national leadership that has the power to control and discipline a national party. Mr. Chrétien, the Liberals and the Red Book are all of a piece. Of course, there *were* promises in politics, lots of them. But these were promises in the sense of patronage, promises of cushy jobs and fat contracts. And a cynic will ask, has anything changed? The answer, I think, is both yes and no. As noted earlier, despite the "spiritual" aspect of *promise*, the notion also has a very decided material side—all that land God promised to Abraham, and all those hockey skates and fancy running shoes you've given your kids for Christmas. Patronage and promise are indissolubly linked. Moreover, I think there's no doubt that this early era of Canadian politics, so rife with patronage, has left an indelible stamp on what politics in general—and political promises in particular—has come to mean for us. Governments exist to hand out goodies, whether jobs, bridges or "benefits," and that's what many political promises are still about.

But *promise* means something more than this.

Political promises, in the modern era, have become fundamental to articulating the differences between parties and politicians, and establishing competing political visions for the country: the word, as well as the idea, is now a major term in our political vocabulary. But this side of promise was slower in developing. A case in point is the great debate around conscription, an issue which tore the country apart from 1916 to 1945; indeed, Mackenzie King's promise not to bring in conscription, ultimately reversed by the plebiscite of 1942, makes Mr. Chrétien's problems with the GST seem very small by comparison. King, of course, was faced with a very real problem. In both world wars, the political and military authorities had expected hostilities to come to a rapid conclusion, so that the Canadian contribution would be small and could be made up entirely of volunteers. But things didn't quite work out that way; by 1916 in WWI, and 1941 in WWII, it was clear that these respective wars were going to run on a while. But both wars were fought in Europe, and our particular connection to them was through the United Kingdom—and defending "the English" was not an obviously popular cause in Quebec. The first time around, Robert Borden, the Conservative prime minister, brought in conscription, though virtually every French-speaking MP voted against it: and from that time forward, the Conservative Party has had a hard time in Quebec. In the end, fewer than 25,000 conscripted men were sent overseas, but when King's turn came to face the problem, he was understandably cautious. He first committed himself against conscription, at least for overseas service, but as the apparent need for it rose, held a referendum to get him out of his promise. It was defeated, overwhelmingly, in Quebec, but succeeded because of its support in the other provinces. Finally, conscription was implemented (though once more it was of only minor practical consequence), again dividing the country—though less so than in the First World War. In all this, "promise" didn't play quite the role in the debate that we might expect today. Certainly, King's government—no less than Chrétien's—had "promised" not to introduce conscription, and, interestingly, the standard (and superb) history of this great debate is called *Broken Promises*.[4] But the title, I'd say, is anachronistic, a projection of our own feelings back into that period. The conscription debates, though fiery enough, were framed in a different emotional context (the French versus the English, nativists against imperialists) and the particular emotional resonance of *promise* wasn't that prominent. The word "promise" was used, but it wasn't the *defining* word. "Commitment" was more common, or the sort of language that Mackenzie King used in the House, introducing the National Resources Mobilization Act, which created conscription for home defence: "The bill to be introduced today in no way affects the raising of men to serve in the armed forces overseas. Once again I wish to repeat my *undertaking*, frequently given, that no measure for the conscription of men for overseas service will be introduced by the present administration."[5] Serious political discourse still employed language—and assumed an emotional context—that was largely parliamentary. For a man like King, promises really did mean patronage, and weren't, in a larger sense, taken seriously. As Louis St. Laurent—one of the survivors of the King era—put it, "An election promise, after all, is a mere cream puff of a thing, with more air than substance in it."[6]

St. Laurent made this remark during the 1957 election campaign, which of course he lost to John Diefenbaker. And it's with Diefenbaker, I think, that we first see *promise* in something like its modern sense. In fact, John Diefenbaker was the first modern Canadian politician.

This statement seems amazing, I know. As a boy, I met Mr. Diefenbaker many times—he would come striding along Sussex Street, where I'd be waiting to catch my bus to Lisgar Collegiate—and often enough, on these occasions, he would be wearing a homburg hat; indeed, he was the only human being I have ever met to do so. Nonetheless, he *was* modern. Most substantially, he was modern in the sense that it was his generation of politicians who took over from leaders who'd seen the country, in fact the world, through the Second World War: St. Laurent and C.D. Howe gave way to Diefenbaker; Duplessis to Paul Sauvé, then Lesage; Eisenhower to Kennedy; Anthony Eden and Macmillan to Harold Wilson. But Diefenbaker was also modern in a more limited, tactical sense. Above all, he was the first Canadian politician to use television effectively. By today's standards, his television style was much too "hot," but the medium was young then, and he had an extraordinary ability to *look into* the camera, and connect with the people on the other side. What he said wasn't especially convincing, and was scarcely meant to be. *He* was convincing. *He* was believable—few actors, after all, have more completely immersed themselves in a part. And because he was believable, he became someone to *believe in.*

Instinctively, John Diefenbaker understood the dynamics of modern politics—or at one level he did—and *promise* was part of this. It wasn't so much the particular promises he made, or the politics they embodied (did he have a politics? did Kennedy?) as the emotional and psychological field in which they operated. His promises were definitely, if not explicitly or

coherently, connected to a *vision*—the aspect of politics that
gave George Bush such difficulty—and defined a leadership that
was largely personal and moral. Diefenbaker, of course, was a
very intelligent man; he even had areas of real competency. But
this had nothing to do with his political success; it was his passion, sincerity, his self-evident good-heartedness—all melded
into his personal style—that brought him victory: it was purely
personal. Indeed, since Diefenbaker, no national government
has succeeded for long by defining itself in terms of competency,
management, "the team." With Diefenbaker, we can see the
development of a new political rhetoric, a quite different way of
talking about politics. And, interestingly, part of that rhetoric
was a calculated nostalgia that reached back and helped invent
our beloved small-town language of *platforms* and *planks*. People
like Preston Manning and Mike Harris exploit this today, but
Diefenbaker invented it. Diefenbaker was the first Canadian
prime minister to do most of his travelling by plane, his com-
municating by television—but he was also the first prime minister to grasp the evocative appeal of speaking from the back of
a railway car. He defined politics in a new way, and even the past
was a part of it.

As usual—in speaking of him—his peculiar novelty can be
seen most clearly by a reference to Lester Pearson. During the
1958 election, in which Pearson's Liberals were almost
destroyed, Pearson also made his share of promises. In town
after town—where people were looking for a new bridge or a
road or a post office—Pearson would promise it to them, *"when
it becomes economically and politically possible."* This qualification
always fell flat, sometimes elicited boos. A reporter, travelling
with Pearson, asked why he didn't drop it—and Pearson, with

uncharacteristic rudeness, turned and snapped, "Why the hell don't you shut up?"[7] Some people, of course, will take this as an instance of Mr. Pearson's honesty, or proof that he wasn't "polit- ical"—people were always saying this about Pearson. But that's nonsense. Lester Pearson was as political as any former high-level civil servant is bound to be—which is to say, down to his fingertips. It was just that he was political in the old way, the way he'd learned in Ottawa during the forties and fifties. After Diefenbaker, all that had changed.

Looking back at Diefenbaker's era, or Kennedy's, it's easy enough to see that people were looking, generally, for a new promise, something different from the corporate, management style of politics personified by Eisenhower in America and C.D. Howe here. And this was the period in which *promise*, in the fully modern sense, really became important. But where, exactly, did the idea fit into this new political discourse, and why was it so attractive?

First, promises are *familiar* and *universal.*

Political promises—of the simple patronage variety—have been with us for a long time; so the redefinition, and enlargement, of the political promise was an easy evolution.

Even more importantly, promises are a part of everyday life. We all know how they work; they're part of a common, universal vocabulary. The rules and appeal of promise-making cut across regional, class and linguistic boundaries. Different promises appeal to different groups, but everyone understands, in a general way, the discourse of promises. For democratic politicians, in an age of mass communications, there's an obvious advantage here. You *have* to speak to everyone, and in a consistent way. Indeed, the discourse of promise helps cope with a problem, which exists in all democratic societies, which mass communications only exacerbates. In reality, people and groups have very different political interests, but parliamentary democracy relies on the acceptance of a broad, common political framework. The discourse of promises reinforces this—both in reality and as a myth: despite the differences, they can all be dealt with in the same way . . . and if this is true, can the differences be so great?

Secondly, promises make an *emotional* appeal.

As we've seen, promises work by establishing an emotional connection to the voter at the deepest personal and ethical level. We are not convinced by promises; we believe in them. Not only that; we *want* to believe in them, just as we wanted to believe in the promises of our parents. So promises are especially useful to a style of politics that emphasizes the personal; *believe my promises, believe in me.* Politics is moved from a rational and intellectual level to one which is sentimental and symbolic, communicated to voters by the direct appeal of the politician through television.

The advantages here are enormous. Devising an *intellectually* convincing program that can bridge the different interests within mass society is extraordinarily difficult, and indeed, the price of a reasoned, intellectual appeal is invariably electoral failure—as the fate of the NDP demonstrates. No one would want to overestimate the NDP's intellectual depth, but the intellectual heritage of democratic socialism is relatively rigorous in comparison to most modern political ideologies; and supporters of the NDP are often *convinced*, or at least pretend to be. Electorally, though, that conviction has only led to very modest success.

In a sense, all this is a problem of credibility, and as a novelist, I can see an easy analogy. There are two ways you can tell a story—in the first person, or the third. Telling a story in the first person—with an "I" who speaks directly to the reader—has many limitations, but also one great advantage; once the reader is convinced by the narrator, by the voice that's telling the story, the reader will believe anything that voice says. So, as a general rule (of course there are exceptions) the more "incredible" the story, the more attractive a first-person narrator becomes. It is the same with politics, which is now a story told entirely in the first person. There's no longer any attempt to intellectually convince you of the storyline, or even present a logical narrative; rather, you believe in the storyteller. Promises, which are not judged by intellectual criteria, are intrinsic to this.

The third reason for the usefulness of promises is implicit in the first two. Because promise defines political discourse as a personal and emotional discourse, logic, rationality and coherence are all devalued. The old notion of a party "program," some sort of reasoned, coherent response to social reality, now goes by the board, replaced by a Red Book of promises. Issues, which people often complain are not discussed, in fact cease to exist, because ideas with no relation to one another or any factual, analytical context are not ideas at all. They become mere slogans, asserted to provoke an emotional response rather than rational conviction.

But promises also have the advantage of being discreet, separate. And although the modern democratic politician is compelled to speak to everyone at once—and promises give him a way of doing so—promises also allow him to break the audience down into separate parts, to which separate promises can appeal.

The fact that these separate promises don't intellectually add up is simply overlooked. *Promises permit incoherence.*

Judged individually, by largely emotional criteria, we don't ask or expect promises to form a logical whole. Tactically, this is of paramount importance. At any given moment, the majority of the electorate is "decided"—their vote is traditional, split along family, regional, ethnic or linguistic lines. Of course, politicians are concerned with this vote; they certainly want to hold their "traditional" share of it, increase it if they can. But the most important vote is the undecided vote, the "swing" vote; and promises allow politicians to define and *target* this vote. Vast political resources are devoted to this. Polling defines the target; "focus groups" seek to establish particular concerns and desires— and then promises try to appeal to them. And there is a corollary to this, almost more important than the basic principle. As the process of "targeting" the electorate has become more refined, we can now say that *promise* not only permits incoherence, it *encourages* it. Interests grow more and more narrow; promises divide, and subdivide. "Real" divisions in the electorate, as they used to be defined—class is the obvious example—are washed out and replaced by endless groupings and grouplets until the "citizenry" is virtually atomized. Thus, promises, at one and the same time, are global in their appeal and utterly divisive in their effect.

All this, naturally, has profound implications for the nature of political leadership.

For one thing, the possibility of collegial leadership virtually disappears. Promises are personal, and must be made by a person, or at least in a person's name. So leadership becomes largely individual—Diefenbaker, Trudeau, Mulroney define their eras, not the programs they advanced nor, certainly, their cabinets: only historians, thank God, will be compelled to recall "Sinc" Stevens.

At the same time, the definition of the individual and the personal has radically altered. The modern politician, after all, doesn't have to be intellectually convincing—he only needs to establish his credentials in those areas related to promise, his sincerity, his trustworthiness. By the same token, the ability to manage or depth of experience—attributes traditionally associated with leadership—are devalued, or transmuted: thus, within the discourse of promise, intellectual capacity becomes *vision*, careful judgment and close consultation become a negative quality, vacillation, contrasted with *decisiveness.*

As well, a host of other personal qualities, formerly considered private matters, suddenly become relevant issues themselves. John Macdonald was a drunk. Mackenzie King, so far as I understand it, communicated with his dead mother via a dog. But although these men were certainly judged "personally," other *personal* qualities were considered more important than such flaws or quirks in their character; they were judged by their wit, knowledge, persuasiveness, capacity for work. Today we know an astonishing amount about the sexual and family lives of politicians. We have to. Political judgments are increasingly indistinguishable from personal judgments—the discourse of promise, so deeply rooted in our earliest emotional lives, places an inevitable stress upon "family" values. In the last American presidential election, the question was asked: "Who would you want to babysit your kids, Clinton or Dole?" Within the discourse of promise, that is a relevant question. "Character issues" are now the only issues that count.

But leadership is not only redefined, it takes on a new dimension. Promise endlessly divides and subdivides the citizenry until, as a practical matter, it ceases to exist: *it's only united within the personality of the leader himself*; the leader's personality, within the discourse of promise, becomes the only unifying principle available. In short: politics becomes *nothing but* leadership, but leadership becomes *nothing but* personality.

And yet—someone might object—why don't we have a cult of the leader? I would answer: we do—we have a cult of leaders-with-feet-of-clay. In other words, our parents. As we've seen, our most important promises are made with God and with children, and it's apparent, as this is projected into feelings about political leadership, where the emphasis lies. We no longer see politicians as gods, and ourselves as faithful subjects—promise, politically, is now more securely rooted within the family drama. So we don't require our leaders to be heroic. We're more comfortable, as we eat our TV dinners in the family room, with leaders who represent parental figures, warts and all, and if that means we're cast in the role of children, we can at least say that this is more in keeping with a political democracy. Children can protest, whine, sulk. They can even seek about for substitutes; in this day and age, they can probably call the Children's Aid and insist upon them. Leadership once had something in common with generalship; captains of industry were considered legitimate political material. Now, political leadership is an aspect of parenting.

Here, I think, you have the four large sets of reasons why the discourse of promise has been triumphant. It's *familiar*, universal and an easy evolution from previous practice. It's *emotional*—it makes a profound connection to the electorate, and never falls under intellectual scrutiny. It permits and encourages *incoherence* and *division*. And it redefines the *political leader* and his *personality*, turning the political leader into an increasingly symbolic and sentimental figure.

Those are the positive reasons—but, inevitably, there is a negative side to this, even for those politicians who accept and revel in this way of doing politics. Precisely because it taps into the parent-child relationship, and the particular power of those emotions, the possibility of a profoundly negative response always exists. Breaking promises incurs a childish wrath. Moreover, all political promises contain the "big promise"—we'll look after you, *I promise that everything will be all right.* The extravagant nature of this claim is always on the verge of being exposed; when it is, the sense of betrayal is profound. So the discourse of promises provides the democratic politician with a uniquely powerful way of making emotional contact with the electorate, a connection that is unregulated by realistic expectations, and not subjected to rational scrutiny; but this very power, if turned against the politician, can be devastating.

Now, everywhere, *promise* is triumphant; it sets political agendas, defines political personalities. It has revolutionized the way we think, feel and talk about politics. But what effect has it had on our political life?

Simply put, the discourse of promises—by itself, but in combination with other factors as well—has led to an inevitable infantilization of politics. *Political talk is now baby talk.* From every perspective—issues, leadership, the practical conduct of politics—our political life has become increasingly childish, whether one uses the word abusively, or simply descriptively.

In the first place, *promise* assumes and creates infantile expectations and responses in the electorate. The discourse of promise gives the electorate—divided into various groups, fragments, audiences—permission to express their "demands" without considering the needs of other groups or "reality" conceived in any larger sense. The whole thrust of modern political technique exists to find out what people want—so that the modern democratic politicians can *promise* to satisfy those wants. (Pollsters and the leaders of focus groups are like Santa Claus in the Bay or Eaton's: we line up and tell them all our dearest wishes.) Any attempt to qualify this process by an appeal to a larger definition of reality—as in Pearson's phrase, *when it is politically and economically possible*—has long since become laughable.

Accordingly, national issues and debates cease to exist: within the discourse of promise, there's no such thing as a national interest—we can't conceive of such a broad reality. Since the constitution inevitably raises the question of the nation as a whole, we'd rather not talk about it. For years, we avoided the nation's imminent bankruptcy by defining the issue as relevant only to certain special groups (as if everyone in the country doesn't pay interest) but of course we have no choice: now, by definition, *all* issues must be seen that way. Some issues, of course, *are* special, to a degree limited: agriculture, for example. There are very few farmers in Canada today, and their concerns are, obviously, somewhat regionalized in the West; nonetheless, agriculture remains an extremely important industry in this country. But the idea that an urban, eastern intellectual such as myself might be interested in the problems of my fellow citizens in Melville or Bienfait (pronounced, of course, *bean-fate*) is no longer imaginable—because, in the discourse of promises, "citizenship" only exists within quotes, as if the notion was vaguely suspicious. So national issues have disappeared; at best, they persist as vague, "ethical" benchmarks—the environment, for example—which function largely as touchstones for the "sincerity" of the political leader.

And what of our leaders? They seem to occupy some peculiar, ambiguous position, declassed, downwardly mobile, though still with the trappings of some former, grander status. They are now too familiar to be heroic, and yet, unavoidably, they exercise peculiar power over us. Vaguely, it seems, we remember who they are, but we no longer *think* much about them, no longer attempt to understand or judge their accomplishments. Emotions and cacophony swirl around them, as if—in some modern, divided family with siblings and step-siblings, and figures even less well defined—they were presiding at an unruly breakfast table, everyone in a rush to meet their own agenda. Do we *like* them? That, apparently, is the only relevant question we still ask: as if they were characters in a situation comedy, some rerun in the afternoon.

Which, I suppose, is a reasonable reflection of who and where we are.

Chapter Three

—◄o►—

Model Promises

*P*romise is deeply rooted in our culture, and in ourselves, part of the emotional lives of each of us. Above the law and beyond accountability, dependent on faith and expressing our most profound hope for the future, it defines a closed psychological and ethical system. Politically, it is now our dominant form of discourse, shaping political agendas and defining political leadership. In general, it constitutes an *infantilization* of politics, for it's purely emotional, eschewing the rational and coherent, and is ultimately egotistical, seeking to break the electorate down into smaller and smaller groupings. Again, it defines a closed world—or at least tries to exclude any world outside the self—and refuses all realistic constraint.

Obviously, this is not a purely Canadian phenomenon. We can see it everywhere, or at least everywhere in the West. Its appeal is universal in modern, mass democracies. At one and the same time, it allows politicians to speak a universal language, and yet break their electorates down into particular "targets." Because of its deep emotional resonance, it's especially effective at reaching the individual through television and the mass media. And it allows the development of a politics which is focused on the leader, and tolerates, indeed encourages, incoherence in policy and program.

But the general dominance of promise is not simply the reason it has been so successful here. We may not have invented it, but our own politics has shaped it in crucial ways. The discourse of promise has distinctly Canadian aspects because it's modelled on particular Canadian realities.

What are those models? Why has this particular way of looking at, thinking of and talking about politics been so successful here?

But I think I should ease you into this . . .

I

The reader will have gathered that I live in Ottawa, was indeed born and raised here. To you, this city is the capital of Canada, the background to Peter Mansbridge's solemnities. But for me the vast machinery of the federal government, the acres of grotesquely ugly buildings, the great rivers of traffic that move the bureaucrats between them, the periodic disruptions of daily life at the behest of the security forces, merely constitute a surreal imposition on normal activity. This is actually a real place, where we do real things, like cut trees, peddle fuel oil, write computer software, build boats in the garage. We, after all, know how to pronounce North Gower. Of course we're a capital, but of the Ottawa Valley, or the *Outaouais.*

Growing up here, the federal government was naturally a presence, but in a wholly domestic way. For example, I can remember playing ball hockey one day, when a large limousine, passing along Thomas Street, disrupted our game. As usual, we stepped to one side, chucked a few snowballs. But the limousine stopped and a shadowy hand, behind the window, waved us to carry on. We did so—and for the next ten minutes, a smile occasionally flickering across his face, Vincent Massey, the Governor General, enjoyed a respite from affairs of state.

So the government has always been *there*, but the centre of this town was certainly *not* the Parliament Buildings. They existed merely as a place where one took one's cousins when they visited, and as a source of revenue for the Connaught Restaurant. The *real* centre—Ottawa being no different from any other Canadian city in this respect—was the railway station, Ottawa Union. Rising above the Rideau Canal, occupying the southern side of Confederation Square—with a fine old railway hotel, the Château Laurier, directly opposite—it was here that you could find the real Ottawa, for it was full of odd characters. Like other Canadian train stations, it was a sort of industrial cathedral, suffused with a vague, holy light, and full of strange echoes: a place of mystery, secrets, the antecedents to journeying. I remember especially the tunnel, leading out of it, that ran under Confederation Square to the Château, and how your steps echoed and rang as you walked, so that a trip to pick up *The New York Times* turned into a clandestine expedition.

I wonder if that tunnel is still there. Probably. But of course the station, *as* a station, no longer exists. The trains have long since been exiled to the suburbs, the tracks along the canal ripped up, replaced with a park. Nonetheless, they couldn't actually pull the old station down. That would have been too great a desecration, even for the brutes who make these sorts of decisions. It's still there, all right, but it's been transformed. The old bronze doors at the front are no longer used, and you go in the side, which is now as gussied up as the Glebe; and a proud sign reads, *National Conference Centre.* For the old station, renovated and refurbished, has moved from my little domestic stage to a greater one. It's now home to the various conclaves, confabulations and parleys hosted by the federal government. But one in particular forms its true *raison d'être: The First Ministers' Conference.* And so the perceptive reader will now understand that the foregoing charming memoir of the capital was written solely to induce him, and seduce her (if I may be politically correct and incorrect at one and the same time) into the contemplation of a horror. I mean, of course, *federal-provincial relations.*

But there's nothing for it.

Remember, we're looking for the Canadian models that lie behind *promise,* and surely in federal-provincial relations, and especially the First Ministers' Conference, we have a perfect mirror—an unruly, ill-mannered, loudmouthed assemblage presided over by a *pater familias* grown uncertain and hesitant, full of ambiguity: an accurate enough reflection of the early-morning breakfast nook in most suburban households.

Which is fun. But the spectacle of federal-provincial relations, as it lurches between farce and terminal boredom, is in fact serious business. This seriousness affects us in many ways, but it especially relates to *promise* by establishing and legitimizing certain crucial structural elements which allow this discourse to take place. The relationship between the provinces, symbolized and represented by their premiers, and the federal government, in the person of the prime minister, defines a whole way of doing politics in Canada.

The correspondence of this model to *promise* is clear enough: the premiers are a clutch of kids, while the feds are, or at least pretend to be, adult. Take the premiers first. Infinitely aggrieved, claiming a disenfranchised helplessness in relation to "the feds," they have an endless list of wants and "needs," which for all practical purposes can never be satisfied . . . training programs, health, education, higher education . . . anything, everything. They not only demand a hundred particular promises, they also insist on *the big promise*—to be looked after and taken care of in some absolute way. Accordingly, their "right" to make demands is without condition or limit: children expect their parents to promise *everything*. Although they mouth a rhetoric of "responsibility," this is merely public relations, and only vague forces and fuzzy ideological precepts—"public opinion," "national unity"—constrain them. They try to get away with as much they can, which is usually a lot: kids do.

On the other hand, the federal government is clearly posited as a virtually omnipotent entity, hoping for a godlike status, though usually resigned to a sort of Father-Knows-Best role—"a non-custodial parent" as two journalists have recently put it.[1] Self-defined by several generations of national politicians as the ultimate solution to all our problems—from the provider of jobs, to the defender of the loftiest ethical goals—the federal government's resources are assumed to be infinite, a carcass that can be carved up forever. By now rather trapped in this role, the federal government, nevertheless, refuses to quite give it up. In the end, despite everything, it's too attractive. They need this assumption in order to make their promises credible.

Crucial to this model, of course, is its *irresponsibility*. This is, in a perverse way, constitutionally built into the system, precisely because the contemporary structuring of federal-provincial relations, with its First Ministers' Conferences and Continuing Committees and endless secretariats, is not mentioned in the constitution at all. This entire structure, *as* a structure, isn't responsible to anything or anybody.

47

Of course, provincial and federal politicians are "responsible"; they're elected. But they're elected to the House of Commons in Ottawa, or the provincial legislatures from Victoria to St. John's—not the old railway station on Confusion Square. And only occasionally—even if you're thinking of Quebec—does their performance on this antic stage count much with their own electorates. Did anyone vote for Ralph Klein because they thought he would "stand up" to Ottawa? I doubt it. At least once, René Lévesque's performance—he was outdone by Trudeau—may have cost him provincially, but in all their campaigns the PQ has run on a promise of "good government," in which fed-bashing is only an incidental element. Just because of this political irresponsibility, federal-provincial conferences can accomplish very little: as is always true in the discourse of promise, there's no accountability, everything is dependent on faith.

Of course, behind the scenes there is substance, because the serious talk is all about money. But it only compounds the irresponsibility, because federal-provincial financing agreements are themselves irresponsible. Don't worry—I won't even attempt to explain this extraordinary labyrinth of bloc grants, conditional grants and tax points. And there's no need, for the basic rules of this game (game!) are clear enough: you try to get the other guy to raise taxes that pay for programs you've promised your electorate. Let there be no mistake, by the way; this works both ways. The federal government has been quite happy, over the years, to promise programs the provinces must implement—and then quietly back away from the financing arrangements designed to support them. And the provinces, when it comes to the federal government, ceaselessly try to play Oliver Twist:

more, more, more . . . more money, more power, more every-thing. Promises to provincial electorates that require federal money—promises by the feds that the provincial governments must carry out—broken promises that are never your fault but always someone else's: at this point, all previous metaphors for *promise* can be abandoned—it's just a nasty can of worms.

In its separate elements, the mirroring of promise in federal-provincial relations is clear enough. But you have to be careful; to a degree, this actually demonstrates the reverse of what I want to show here. That is, I expect that federal-provincial relations have gradually acquired these qualities *from* promise, rather than the other way around, though today the process is clearly self-reinforcing. This is partly a historical question. Just as political promises have a long history before what I'm calling *the discourse of promise*, so contemporary federal-provincial relations are the result of a complex historical evolution. The first line of this evo-lution is essentially constitutional, and its earlier part was largely juridical in nature, involving a series of legal cases, many appealed to the Judicial Committee of the Privy Council—the highest legal authority of British Imperialism. The consequence of that history was an extraordinary expansion of provincial power, far beyond anything the original designers of Confeder-ation had ever contemplated. They had drafted the British North America Act to provide for a very strong central govern-ment, mindful that a looser federalism in the United States had produced the Civil War, then just bloodily concluded. Indeed, there's evidence that John Macdonald actually believed that the provinces would eventually disappear, and Canada would become a unitary state. But the British Law Lords, especially Viscount Haldane, quickly put an end to that possibility. Decision after decision shifted more and more power to the provinces. The surprising point about this power shift, at least for most Canadians today, is that it had little to do with Quebec. The key decisions (naturally, lawyers will argue ceaselessly about this) involved Ontario and Alberta, and the issues which we now associate with Quebec weren't much in evidence. The reason for this was simple enough. Without worrying about "distinct society" or "special status" the British North America Act quietly recognized that Quebec was "different" by guaranteeing Quebec's civil code, providing for particular representation from Quebec on the Supreme Court, and absolutely protecting Quebec's educational system (which was then denominational). The importance of these decisions was twofold. On the one hand, they opened the way for a looser and more conflict-ridden national politics. But—even more importantly—the interpretation of the constitution took it so far from its original intent and introduced so many anomalies into it, that it ceased to be very useful as a basic document organizing national affairs. So this evolution, taken as a whole, positively invited the development of parallel structures of a quasi-constitutional nature. Put another way: the disjunction between intent, interpretation and practice in the constitution was itself a kind of incoherence, encouraging incoherence generally. This would ultimately be of paramount importance to the discourse of promise. But that lay in the future; this early history took place in a context quite different from the one essential to promise; it was less charged, less emotional, the public was less involved.

The second line of evolution was financial, and is more recent. Indeed, federal-provincial relations, as we know them today, really begin to take shape with the passage, in 1961, of an innocuous-sounding piece of legislation, the Federal-Provincial Fiscal Arrangements Act (1961). With this measure, the last trace of the federal government's wartime usurpation of taxing powers ended, and all the provinces began collecting taxes across the board. Before that point—from 1941—the federal government had collected the bulk of the nation's taxes, rebating money to the provinces under a variety of formulas. This system enhanced federal power, but it meant that the federal government was seen as the sole tax collector, while the provinces received credit for most of the popular programs the taxes funded. The 1961 legislation (passed by Diefenbaker's government) was meant to reverse that—in other words, it was at this point that "the game of fiscal federalism" began in earnest.

Although it's important to remember that other factors and problems were involved, it was the rise of modern Quebec nationalism (or, more exactly, its change from nationalism to *étatisme*) that now drew these two lines of evolution together. Responding to the rise of separatism, Lester Pearson organized a number of federal-provincial conferences, under the general rubric of "co-operative federalism," which established federal-provincial relations in a completely contemporary setting—which is to say, my old train station. Under the glare of television lights, with commentators babbling off-camera and leaks spilling out of the backrooms, the nation's fundamental business was transacted. As all this was played out, they took on much of the character of *promise*, which was developing in any case. But they also made a great contribution *to* the discourse of promise, in two crucial ways.

First, federal-provincial relations, as a system—*as a structure* —is self-contained, self-sufficient, self-referential. That is the real meaning of its irresponsibility. On the one hand, it reproduces the closed emotional world of childhood and the family—the world in which *promise* first evolves; on the other, it constitutes a theological system, mimicking the intellectual order in which it is most carefully elaborated. Any reality outside itself is quickly excluded or very greatly diminished. It is, quite simply, unreal.

That is the contribution of the *structure* of federal-provincial relations. But its content and internal workings make a contribution too. Above all, it legitimates a division, and *dividing*, as a fundamental political moment: it legitimates the division and incoherence which was intrinsic to its development. *Promise* takes this division, and multiplies it endlessly; but this is where it legitimately begins.

Of course, some will immediately object that this is silly. Unreal? Theological? Surely, in discussions of federal-provincial financing arrangements, you reach the very acme of *the economically and politically possible* in terms of this country. Yes: *but only within the terms established by the system itself.* It's a closed system, defining its own reality, but cut off from any other—a strange, science-fiction, parallel universe. Only within such a world—to take merely one example—could the question of whether French-speaking federal bureaucrats, as opposed to French-speaking provincial bureaucrats, have control over manpower training, be seen, *by anyone*, as somehow crucial to the integrity of Quebec. It's pure Alice in Wonderland. We're right in the middle of that old joke, the one about the international essay competition on the theme of the elephant. The Brit writes on "The Elephant and Empire"; the French entry is entitled "*L'Amour et l'éléphant*"; and the Canadian turns in a paper called "The Elephant: A Federal or Provincial Responsibility?"

This sort of thing captures the unreality of the whole business well enough. It's full of ironies. This astonishing, arcane structure, which has evolved in no small part at the insistence of the province of Quebec, is now one of the more rational reasons the separatists advance for departing the country; certainly, the system is utterly beyond reformation. Of course people try. I've defined it as "irresponsible," and so have many, many others before me. Periodically, therefore, someone suggests *making* it responsible, perhaps by incorporating First Ministers' Conferences into the constitution. But such notions never come to anything, and never will. If you have a grasp of reality—chemistry, say, or physics—you can't engage in a reasoned discussion with an alchemist, or someone intent on building a perpetual motion machine. It's the same here.

Moreover, no one truly does want to change it; the irresponsibility and ineffectiveness of the system are precisely the reason for its appeal. This *is* a perpetual motion machine. No problem is ever solved; no question cannot be reopened. It can go on forever. And the armies of bureaucrats and politicians, federal and provincial—who staff the secretariats, prepare the working papers, conduct the endless negotiations—are like the last surviving speakers of a long-dead language; they'll do anything to keep it going. The language which they *don't want to speak* is Canadian.

But neither do we, the electorate. We too find advantage in this unreality. It legitimates an utterly unreal world, without checks, in which—like the provinces—we can ask for, and expect to be promised, anything.

But our irresponsibility, let's be clear, is not a moral defect. Since this is a *political* system, our relationship to it takes a particular *political* form, has a particular *political* definition. This consists in a *divided* identity, which permits a split and constantly shifting relation to this whole process. Simply put, it allows us a kind of ghostly provincial "citizenship" along with our nationality as Canadians. We are Albertans—and Canadians. Newfies—and Canadians. Quebecers—and Canadians. But the real basis for this division within ourselves evaporates, day by day. In fact, we all live in Canada. Indeed, we all live, at the very least, in North America—increasingly, as a practical matter, in the western world. At an accelerating rate, the dynamics of modernism are washing away the real bases of all local identity; fewer Canadians die where they were born—half the people in Calgary, God knows, probably lived in Toronto last year. And since our individual identities are, in part, tied to our local identity, we find this process threatening. Of course this problem is especially acute in Quebec. But this is only a matter of degree. The dynamic of western modernism is an English-speaking dynamic—most schoolchildren in France will speak better English than our prime minister—and that places an obvious pressure on people whose individual identities are expressed in French. But it's also a liberal, secular and universalizing dynamic, so the Canadian West, with strong conservative religious traditions, developed in a region with a special geographic identity, feels it too.

What is our response to these realities? Well, we'd rather not face them; everywhere, people try to insist on what they are losing. At a time when the rational basis of localism is disappearing, localism becomes all the rage. Even an attempt to consolidate the government of Metro Toronto faces this kind of opposition—people suddenly rally to the defence of local administrations, for which a majority have probably never even troubled to vote.

At one level—and this is very close to the heart of federal-provincial relations—this all rests on a fairly elementary confusion between the possibilities and advantages of *administrative* versus *political* decentralization. Local government has always been justified on the ground that it's "close to the people." But in the age of television, jet aircraft and the high-speed modem this rationale is increasingly dubious. I deal with a host of governments—I pay taxes to half a dozen—which are of varying degrees of "remoteness" to me in the political sense; as a practical matter, however, they are all at the other end of the telephone, and effectively merge into a single, Hydra-headed beast. The sensitivity of governments to my "local" situation actually bears no relationship to their political distance from me at all. I'm not sure that I wouldn't rather deal with the GST people— the federal government; administratively located, I believe, in Summerside, P.E.I.—than I would the snow-removal people in the City of Ottawa. Or are they part of the Regional Municipality of Ottawa Carleton? Who knows? Who really cares? They all collect taxes, they all have phone numbers. And whether considered in terms of effectiveness or rudeness, they're pretty much on a par.

Rationally, I know this. We all do. And yet there is an atavistic, immature side of myself that hangs on to a hard kernel of local identity. The little memoir of Ottawa with which I began expresses a positive side of this well enough; we may all live in a greater world, but we all come from somewhere, some very particular place. But—much more important—there's a negative side as well: fears, hostilities, ancient hatreds, resentments. God, how I hate Toronto. And the Ontario government . . . close to me? You have to be out of your mind: they've been building, or rather *not* building, Highway 416 since before I was born. So far as the Ontario government is concerned, the world ends at Steeles Avenue. In fact, let me tell you . . .

But I better cut myself off. You will take my point, in any case. The bizarre world of federal-provincial relations legitimates, and reinforces, this immaturity, this *division*, which is part of my own political identity, and is a crucial element in the discourse of promise. I get to have it both ways, *all* ways. I even get to be adult, mature, Canadian. When I see provincial politicians being, well, *provincial*, I can become, as it were, my national self, and tell them to stop being so childish, and start dealing with the problems of a great continental nation—precisely the problems my immature, childish self works so hard to avoid.

II

Growing up in Ottawa, my childhood suffered one great disruption—and, appropriately enough, this was caused by politics.

John Diefenbaker's victories in 1957, and especially in 1958, owed a good deal to Maurice Duplessis, the premier of Quebec, who'd thrown the Union Nationale electoral machine behind the Conservative cause, providing them with a good deal of their margin of victory. As a reward, Mr. Diefenbaker agreed to shift a number of federal institutions, including the Queen's Printer and the National Film Board, to Quebec. And since my father worked for the NFB, this created a major upheaval in our family life. The Board moved to Montreal. After considerable agonizing—in one of those "temporary" solutions, which turn out to be more or less permanent—my father went with them, commuting between Ottawa and Montreal every weekend. But periodically the direction of this journeying was reversed, and on one memorable occasion, I went off alone to spend the weekend with him. I took the train, of course, and found myself seated beside a man who hailed, I believe, from Saskatoon. He seemed pleasant enough, and certainly looked sane. And I don't quite know how it happened—perhaps I pointed out a passing freight—but very rapidly he shifted the conversational topic to one previously unknown to me, *freight rates*, and proceeded to acquaint me with his views on the subject, held with considerable passion, until we finally arrived in *la métropole*. It was an astonishing monologue. I did my best to keep up, here and there finding something to hang on to—an obsession with the Crowsnest Pass (at least I knew where it was), a vitriolic hatred for Bay Street (which, already loathing Toronto, I quickly assented to). But it was many years before I really understood what he was talking about (or was able to relate it to my own situation on that train—how many *western* premiers have received such plums as the NFB for their political support?). In any case, this was also my personal introduction to *hinterland politics*, which creates a second element in the Canadian model of *promise*.

Hinterland politics is exactly what it says: the politics of the remote parts of the country, at least viewed from the perspective of its metropolitan centres. It's rural politics, small-town politics—the politics of local and regional identity. We normally think of it as being *provincial* as opposed to national or federal; but, in fact, this kind of politics is very much a part of provincial politics itself. The West may be the hinterland of Canada, but so is the B.C. Interior in opposition to Vancouver, or northern and eastern Ontario versus the Golden Horseshoe, or the Gaspé and the Saguenay in relation to Montreal. Mike Harris, the current premier of Ontario, is usually considered "right wing," but his conservative ideology only masks his hinterland roots. Growing up in North Bay, he sees the Ontario government as a vehicle to organize the movement of wealth and opportunity from his part of the world to Toronto—and so it's not surprising that one of his first major acts as premier was a bill to cut Toronto down to size.

Fundamentally, this is not an *ideological* politics: on the contrary, it often views "politics" and political ideas with suspicion; it ultimately seeks its justification in other terms. Typically, hinterland political movements begin *outside* of politics—in the "social gospel" of J.S. Woodsworth and Tommy Douglas that lay behind the CCF, or Bill Aberhart's gospel preaching which laid the basis for Social Credit—and politicization is often a last, reluctant step. Aberhart, for example, offered his movement to several other political parties before starting a party of his own. Invariably, this politics has a strong *negative* aspect—"protest" suggests it well enough—and its leadership is often found among renegades, mavericks, opportunists, political crackpots and eccentrics: "Wacky" Bennett, Bouchard, both the Mannings, Réal Caouette and, of course, Diefenbaker (arguably the greatest hinterland politician of them all). Almost all of these leaders started politics somewhere else, and then "crossed the floor" or otherwise migrated away from the major parties; and they always defined themselves, not in positive terms, but *against*.

Against . . . what?

In the end, *against the metropolis*. The "metropolis," of course, has different definitions: Toronto to Ontarians, Montreal to Quebecers—but the most important is *central Canada* or just "the East." This abstraction, vividly alive in the Canadian West, links Quebec and Ontario into an imperialistic unity, out to rape and pillage the western farmer, oilman, etc.

Canada has thrown up dozens of hinterland groups, from every region of the country, though we normally think of them as originating in the West. But one of the true hotbeds for hinterland politics in Canada has been the Saguenay–Lac St. Jean region of Quebec. This is the area that gave birth to Réal Caouette's *Créditistes*, and it's gone on to become one of the strongest *Péquiste* sections of the province—and of course it's where Lucien Bouchard comes from. Bouchard is actually a typical hinterland politician, though it will no doubt surprise people to consider him that way. It shouldn't. The Saguenay is typical of the regions that produce this sort of politics. The land—"The Kingdom of the Saguenay"—was being mythologized in Cartier's time, and its dramatic beauty makes this easy enough to do. It certainly *is* a hinterland; it was only opened for settlement about 150 years ago, and the first passable road to Quebec City wasn't built until 1951. Its *people* are remarkably homogeneous, and profoundly committed to this particular corner of Quebec. Lucien Bouchard's immediate family is large; in the area, immense. In his memoir, *On the Record*,[2]* he writes: "I use the term *family* in

---

* Rather than irritating the reader's eye, I've consolidated page references into a single endnote. At a couple of points, I've also included a phrase from M. Bouchard's French text in square brackets where I felt it might be useful.

its broadest sense. Grandfathers, grandmothers, uncles, aunts, and cousins were but the first circle. Great-uncles, great-aunts, and second cousins were also a part of our everyday life. I am always surprised to meet people who are unable to name relatives beyond their immediate families." The family, to M. Bouchard, was a "cult"; the family homestead "a shrine"; the ground it stood on "holy." The remarkable people who've built their lives on that holy ground have created for themselves a genuine culture—very narrow and limited, but truly felt. At the centre was religion and language: M. Bouchard was learning to read from *L'Action Catholique* at the age of five, and his later education was in the hands of lay brothers, then the Oblates (and for both he has nothing but praise). His whole family, he writes, "loved and respected beautiful language; they would have had nothing but contempt for *joual*, an urban Quebec dialect." In this last clause, we see the typical hinterland view of the metropolis; but then the Saguenay was truly a world of its own, largely cut off from the rest of the province, and almost happy to get along without it. M. Bouchard's father drove a delivery truck, and loved to take his kids along. "We would travel up and down the streets of Jonquière, Kénogami, Arvida, *and sometimes even Chicoutimi.*" In fact, the great rivalry—in hockey and in scholastic achievement—was between Jonquière and Chicoutimi (which are about fifty kilometres apart). As an adolescent, Bouchard made it as far as Quebec City on a school outing, but doesn't seem to have reached Montreal until he was in his twenties. Indeed, arriving at Laval when he was twenty-one, he found Quebec "a large city." This was 1959—the Quebec capital's population was 171,000, about 100,000 less than Ottawa, where I was growing up. And of course Ottawa never struck me as large, since I was so often in Toronto and Montreal. As Bouchard points out, however, "our people have always been aware of their isolation and its cost" (and whether it's a cost or a benefit, you'll note the *our people*). There was a determined effort, in M. Bouchard's family, to overcome it. The great family sin was "faire simple"— to act or be "simple," a difficult phrase to translate, for it's not quite *hick* or *bumpkin*, though it has a little of both. Regardless, M. Bouchard takes great pride in being a *bluet* (as inhabitants of the area are called) and makes no apology for it: "We often talk about the pride of the Saguenay–Lac St. Jean. I am aware these days that references to Quebec pride are suspect to some, generally the same people who make faces whenever they hear a phrase like 'the regions of Quebec,' immediately thinking of creeping regionalism. The truth of the matter is that regions do exist and they have never stopped feeding metropolitan Montreal . . . Pride in Lac St. Jean and the Saguenay is legitimate."

Here you have a genuine and vigorous regionalism, defining itself against the metropolis—almost ripe for politicization, one might say. All that's required is "alienation." Sticking with M. Bouchard's memoir, it typically makes its first appearance as a general criticism of politics, muddled into the same paragraph where M. Bouchard talks of local pride:

> Pride in Lac St. Jean and the Saguenay is legitimate. People are proud to have survived on their own. They enjoy recalling the names of their fellow citizens who have become successful at home or elsewhere, in business, sports and the arts. They have a traditional distrust of government, which, except for the Union Nationale, admittedly ignored them. Politicians remembered them only to bestow on *les Anglais* some timber limits,

permit them to flood farmlands, or hydroelectric rights on their rivers. And people in our families still remember how some of our grandfathers or great-uncles, during the Great Depression, refused to be on the dole or returned their old-age security cheques.

Here, the "outside" "exploiting" group is defined in essentially racial terms, which is not actually necessary in hinterland politics, though the level of vitriol often reaches that pitch. In this case, of course, that is unquestionably how the "simples" of the Saguenay saw the owners and managers of the pulp-and-paper mills (and other business interests) in the area; and despite his education, M. Bouchard apparently hasn't found any other suitable analytical categories. Indeed, intellectually, he is a loyal *bluet*. "Curiously enough," he goes on, "there was no acrimony towards English-speaking managers, no doubt because the Quebec temperament is not a vindictive one." One would like to pass this sort of thing off as a mere turn of phrase, but it's fundamental to M. Bouchard's view of the world. So I have to point out the obvious. *Curiously enough,* there is no such thing as "the Quebec temperament" and people in *la belle province* are neither more nor less vindictive than anyone else; which is to say, they're very vindictive indeed. So here is the truth behind M. Bouchard's blarney:

The Saguenay was (is) a resource hinterland. It was developed (as such) by large corporations, Canadian, American and multinational, who managed their businesses in English, the dominant business and technical language in the western world, and also one of the chief languages of Protestantism. How did the inhabitants of the area—French-speaking, Catholic, agricultural, steeped in a local identity—respond to this? Well, they responded exactly as M. Bouchard has responded, as most "simple" people would: *they hate the English.*

And this, of course, is the firm bedrock on which M. Bouchard's politics rests.

We can trace this theme out (and get a sense of its depth) by following M. Bouchard's career a little further, as he departed, however briefly, the Saguenay. For example, at Laval, he met and befriended Brian Mulroney—who was *not* an *"Anglais"* but "Irish to the bone." Again, this phrase in not merely literary; Bouchard means it seriously—he's drawing a distinction which he sees as real and important: "[Mulroney] knows injustice exists—and that for a very long time it struck *his own people* very harshly. I always felt that deep down he felt the same way as a French-speaking Québécois would if he lost his language and culture. Deprived of primordial loyalties, he stood alone . . ." etc. etc.

Of course, this is nonsense, the sort of nonsense intrinsic to this sort of thinking. Brian Mulroney is a Canadian; no doubt, he's proud of his family's origins—but the Irish are not *his own people* any more than the Poles, equally long-suffering, are Peter Gzowski's. A simple proof of this was that Mr. Mulroney did not become a Fenian or a Sinn Feiner, but a member of the Progressive Conservative Party of Canada, in fact a very ambitious one, and *because of this he worked hard to improve his French*; according to M. Bouchard, he didn't speak it well when he began at Laval. "He set about learning it with such eagerness and application that he made rapid progress. He was never offended when people corrected him, and was always searching for new words and expressions, which he would try out at the first opportunity." The two young men "came to know each other well, walking and talking in the old town, he improving his French, *while I obstinately refused to speak English because I was paralyzed with shame because of my ignorance."*

Why this refusal and shame? Because, to M. Bouchard, speaking English was an acknowledgment of, and acquiescence in, a subordination to the *Anglais* business owners and managers of the Saguenay—you know, those flooders of farmlands and appropriators of timber rights toward whom, because of the "Quebec temperament," he doesn't feel any vindictiveness.

But one wants to be very careful here. Clearly, there is a disturbing, ominous side to M. Bouchard's view of the world. Family, blood lines and ethnic background are so important to him; his belief in national "temperament" is so unexamined; phrases like "primordial loyalties" fall so easily from his lips— and he seems quite unaware of the effect they might have on others, or the particular consequences of this kind of thinking in modern history. But then he is a very parochial figure. His view of the world is profoundly rooted in the particular, narrow culture from which he comes; especially its isolation, extraordinary homogeneity, Jansenist Catholicism and general backwardness. And that backwardness can't be ignored. M. Bouchard, for example, began reading the great classics of literature and philosophy at an early age, reading them with a true intellectual and moral passion—in an attempt to escape that backwardness; but with the limited experience of life and culture that his background gave him, he could understand those works only in a particular, limited way, which is why, toward the end of the twentieth century, despite that reading, he was able to mount a public platform and passionately identify himself with something called *la race blanche*—French-Canadian women, according to M. Bouchard, not producing sufficient examples of it. All the same, though this view of the world reflects its narrow origins—and the ultra-nationalist tradition in Quebec—it was no doubt reinforced by real humiliations produced by the organization of Quebec society during M. Bouchard's childhood: a phrase like "paralyzed with shame" refers to a dreadful subjective reality which has historic, concrete, objective correlatives. The fact that it has produced such a narrow view of history, marked by a particular sensitivity to people's ethnic and linguistic background, is not entirely surprising, nor entirely to be laid at M. Bouchard's door.

Even so, there was a terrible irony here. Because Brian Mulroney wasn't the only *Anglais* in M. Bouchard's class; far from it. Conrad Black was there, and Michael Meighen, and George McLaren—and many more. In fact, as soon as M. Bouchard started attending lectures, "one thing struck me *above all else* [*toute de suite*]: the large contingent of anglophones, mainly from Montreal. I soon learned that this had never happened before in the faculty." But Quebec was changing, you see. The Liberal Party—the traditional party of *les Anglais*—had finally gained power, the Quiet Revolution was under way. The "English," or some of them, were shedding their racism, or trying to. For M. Bouchard this was, to say the least, profoundly confusing; one of the fundamental assumptions of his mental outlook was evaporating, like a mist. Of course, it could be re-invented: "Canada" could take the place of *les Anglais*. As M. Bouchard tells the story, his grandfather got up from his death bed "to vote one last time for Duplessis," whom the Bouchard family had always supported. Once the Quiet Revolution began, his grandson was destined to reclaim that heritage.

With this particular example in mind, I want to summarize the most important features of hinterland politics, and explicitly relate them to the discourse of promise.

First, M. Bouchard's separatism, like all hinterland politics, uses the hinterland as the general model for society: it becomes the Promised Land, the promise of tomorrow. When he talks about the "Québécois" he really means "our people"—as he would when talking about the people of the Saguenay. Above all, their homogeneity is projected onto Quebec in general, which is thereby endowed with an almost metaphysical unity; if anything does exist outside this, it's consigned to a dreadful pit of "otherness." M. Bouchard essentially admits this. "Whether I like it or not, history made me Québécois of old stock. Nowadays, one almost has to apologize for this. My roots have struck deep into a small part of this earth. I don't think it is better or richer than others, but it is mine. Some may think that it nourishes outmoded values and isolates me from other Québécois who joined us more recently . . . I do not think so. The particular is reductionist only if it prevents access to the universal. But I want my village to be part of a real country that . . . opens to the outside world, starting with the one that has already settled among us, the ethnic communities." After anointing himself with legitimacy (*Québécois de souche*), M. Bouchard invokes the earth—always so central to this tradition—and his deep roots. Note the ambiguity: is his "small part of this earth" the Saguenay, or Quebec? But of course he means both, and they are the same. His reference to "outmoded values" certainly includes his devotion to the traditional French-Canadian family (despite his difficulties in establishing one) and his Catholicism (despite being divorced): in any case, they acknowledge that he remains a traditionalist, a man of the right. And then he almost admits the truth. The particular, in his case, doesn't *prevent* access to the universal; it is *identical with* the universal. His village isn't part of a real country, it defines the real county (*vrai pays*); outside of this reality is "ethnicity." All hinterland politics is like this, fantastically idealizing—*promising.* George Melnyk finds an ideal west in Métis society; Preston Manning in small-town Alberta. The hinterland home becomes the social ideal, the realizable dream, the great promise.

Second, M. Bouchard's separatism, like all hinterland politics, defines itself *against* the metropolis. M. Bouchard appears exceptional here, because the metropolis is so obviously doubled—Canada and Montreal—but actually this is typical: for behind the "Central Canada" of the western form of this tradition lies Bay Street and Toronto. The metropolis with Bouchard—but also typically—has two salient features; it's oppressive, and antithetical (especially in terms of values) to the hinterland.

Canada, for M. Bouchard, fits the bill quite well. It's more or less "*Anglais*"; and the federal government can be made out as a fair menace, despite the fact that the prime minister is usually from Quebec. And Canada couldn't be more antithetical; M. Bouchard has already declared that Canada is "not a real country" and given his definition of "*un vrai pays*" he is of course entirely right. Canada, since Macdonald shook hands with Cartier, has never sought or valued the kind of homogeneous unity which is the crucial part of M. Bouchard's own "national" conception, and M. Bouchard, throughout his public life, has clearly found Canada bewildering.

Montreal is a little more difficult. It's astonishing, given his position in Quebec, how completely M. Bouchard has been able to avoid the place—which, to declare a prejudice, remains my favourite Canadian city. But then it represents the greatest danger to his politics. For one thing, it's a city—truly, "a large city," therefore intimidating. Moreover, it remains suspiciously "*Anglais*"; and even if not, it's often from here that the economic oppression of the hinterland is organized. Culturally, considered in the pure light that shines from the Saguenay, it appears degenerate—recall his strictures about *joual*; and its intellectual life is suspiciously secular. But the great disaster is its ethnicity; *la métropole* is actually (a touch!) cosmopolitan. This challenges the fundamental assumption of homogeneous, even totalitarian unity, projected from the Kingdom of the Saguenay onto the province as a whole. Ethnicity, in fact, has long been the bane of French-Canadian nationalists—who always fear being defined as "ethnics" themselves, since that's a fate they wish to reserve for other people. "Liberal" separatists always think they can apologize for the outbursts of people like Parizeau and Landry toward "ethnics"; in fact, you can't. For here you can see the very heart and soul of separatism; it must be that way. They are the "other" against which the purity of *les Québécois* is defined. In fact, it's clear that M. Bouchard's Kingdom is rather feudal; at the top, people like himself, *Québécois de souche*, who will no longer have to apologize for their status; then more ordinary Quebecers; then "ethnics"; and, no doubt last, Indians and the Inuit.

And, in principle, all other hinterlands define the metropolis in much the same way, though not usually so elaborately, or with M. Bouchard's peculiar sensitivity to blood lines and ethnicity. But there are always the same elements of repression, remoteness and usually some sort of cultural degeneracy or "looseness." As Preston Manning flies over Toronto at night, he no doubt has to suppress a shudder—thousands of people fornicating madly with the lights on. Mr. Harris—again thinking of Toronto—sees a city grown fat on the cream of Ontario's hinterlands, and cunningly adopts an ideology of trimming the fat.

Finally, but in a way most importantly, there are the *feelings* involved in all this, especially the terrible feeling of abandonment, inferiority, shame and the rage they engender. I've already quoted M. Bouchard, but it has often enough been heard from Mr. Lougheed—and Louis Riel.

In relation to *promise*, hinterland politics provides an interesting contrast to the kind of influence at work in federal-provincial relations. To be sure, both legitimize the division which is such a fundamental part of the discourse of promise. But while federal-provincial relations legitimizes, and draws on, that aspect of *promise* rooted in childhood and familial relations, hinterland politics emphasizes the religious, apocalyptic and eschatological side of the equation. M. Bouchard's holy ground, The Kingdom of the Saguenay, is universalized in Quebec, and projected as the New Jerusalem of Sovereignty—just as western hinterland politicians on the left have projected the New Jerusalem of social justice. Indeed, in the West—going right back to the religious fantasies of Riel—political ambitions have been defined not only in religious language, but in a very extreme religious language, and generations of political leadership have been drawn from men of the cloth: Preston Manning, Manning *père*, Aberhart, Tommy Douglas, Woodsworth. For such men, of course, *promise* is the meat and drink of their soul. Both in Quebec and the West, a sense of exclusion from the centre—from *la métropole*, "the East": always suspect, corrupt, mongrelizing, cosmopolitan—has reinforced a self-definition built around purity and righteousness, expressed in the absolutes of race and language. This has led to a politics of "movements," rather than parties, often embracing the most disparate ideological groups, submerging all differences in the vision of grand, apocalyptic projects: the great promise of justice, sovereignty or some other grand word. Eschewing rationality, it is a politics of odd hybrids and bastards, Orwellian contradictions: a right-wing party called *Reform*, a conservatism that is *progressive*, sovereignty coupled to "association." Within such a world, it seems perfectly reasonable that men like Preston Manning and Lucien Bouchard should be opposite sides of the same coin, for they both, in the end, speak the same language—the language of *promise*.

III

I have been talking about a model—by definition, an abstraction. But we must remember that promises are always specific, concrete. Of course, specific promises may well concern abstractions—a promise of justice, for example—but every promise is separate, particular. Promises are always *about* something. In general, we can say that all promises (like dreams) express a wish, something we want or desire; but, with political promises this wish is almost always felt and expressed as a *need* or *grievance*, and the person or group seeking the promise is, or conceives themselves to be, a *victim*.

And in defining *promise* in Canada, the Canadian Indians[†] have been our archetypal victim, their needs and grievances have

† All terms used to describe people on the basis of race are unsatisfactory, since race itself has virtually no legitimate meaning. "Aboriginal," "Native,"

become the model for all others. Marginalized elsewhere, they are central to the discourse of promise.

Writing about Indians is difficult; conceivably, more nonsense has been written on this theme than any other within the Canadian political firmament. Much of that nonsense has been written by various "experts," a good deal of it by Indians themselves. Most of this is more or less racist, harbouring the quaint belief that Indians are inherently "different." I have known Indians all my life; my wife is part Indian. I am here to tell you: Indians are just like you and me. Of course, some of them *pretend* to be different. When you see Ovide Mercredi on television, he's usually wearing a neat little buckskin jacket; around town, delving into the pasta, it's usually a dark suit—and why not? Since Indians watch as much television as the rest of us, they often believe the most astonishing things about Indian culture and history. For example, many sincerely believe in a set of notions, originating in eighteenth-century French romanticism, that Indians and their cultures are somehow "in harmony" with nature. This is silly. As is true with all hunting and gathering peoples, nature bulked large in traditional Indian mythology and systems of belief; and since all such cultures are characterized by a low order of technological development, their lives had relatively little impact on their natural surroundings. But given the opportunity—by the Hudson's Bay Company, for example—Indians cheerfully helped trap numerous species to the edge of extinction, and

"First Nations" all impose European notions upon people, and cultures, which (at least originally) conceived themselves in very different terms, and are to one degree or another obnoxious. "Indian," at least, has a certain legal clarity, germane to my discussion—for it is the term used to define people covered under the Indian Act.

today insist on legal hunting and fishing rights in defiance of all ecological sense. Traditional Indian culture, of course, is of extraordinary anthropological interest. But since this culture, in all of its manifestations, was preliterate, knew nothing of money and markets, and had no conception of science, it is unlikely to provide much of a guide to people attempting to live at the dawn of the twenty-first century—any more than the traditional culture of the Celts is of much use to Matthew Barrett as he racks up more billions for the Bank of Montreal. Nothing demonstrates this more clearly than Indian history itself. Presented with the advantages of the steel edge, Indians didn't spend much time memorializing the "traditional" virtues of flint: Indians, like most everyone else, have always understood that cultural adaptation was the price of survival. But even to write of *Indian* culture in this way is suspect; the very word is tinged with racism, and imposes, in its generality, a unity upon Indian life that simply didn't exist. Even today, Indian groups are very different, and before European settlement this was even more true—the meeting between an Ojibway and a Tlingit, supposing it ever took place, would have provoked only mutual bewilderment. In their extraordinary variety, and at their different degrees of economic and social development, Canadian Indian cultures demonstrated the full range of human possibility, from sadism to slavery, beauty to ecstasy.

However, bearing all this in mind, there should be no mistake about the fundamental judgment. The treatment of Indians by Canadian governments, at all levels, has been appalling, ranging from the merely paternal to the outright vicious. Since the *degree* of this maltreatment is, in itself, a crucial part of how the Indians' situation relates to *promise*, it's worth noting a few details. Indians "enjoy" standards of health far below those of other Canadians; on average they live seven or eight years less than the rest of us, and their infant mortality rate—we're talking here about dead babies—is double the national figure. The ordinary infectious diseases are no longer the killers they once were; now, the principal cause of death between one and forty-five years of age is some form of violence—accidents, suicides, death by fire and firearms; suicide rates are triple that of the rest of the country. Economically, the situation of Canadian Indians is catastrophic. Most Indians live in poverty. Their incomes are half the national average. Employment rates are the lowest of any ethnic group, and 42 per cent of Indians still rely on social assistance in one form or another. Indians are overrepresented in Canadian prisons by a factor of *seven*. In Centennial Year, only two hundred native students were enrolled in Canadian universities, and though that situation has thankfully improved, educational standards for Indians are still well below the Canadian norms: 8 per cent of Indians have university education, in comparison to 20 per cent of the nation as a whole.[3]

I could go on, but what's the point? Everyone in the country knows that this is a disaster of vast dimensions. And, so far as *promise* is concerned, it is the extent of the disaster which is important. It's *total.* Indians, in Canada, are the *ultimate victims.* Their *objective* condition is so bad that any and all *grievances* are entirely credible. When it comes to grievances and the expression of *need,* Canadian Indians can make virtually any demand.

But those grievances are expressed within a particular context, and here *promise* comes very directly into the picture. Indians routinely express their grievances in terms of promises—*broken* promises. They account for their condition (and that account is given broad credibility) in terms of the repeated and consistent failure of Canadian governments to honour the promises made to Canadian Indians in treaties and other obligations. Arguably, at one level, this account is false. Even if the treaties had been honoured to the letter, that would not necessarily mean that Canadian Indians would be substantially better off today. Still, they'd sure *feel* better about it. In any case, *objectively*, treaties were broken, promises were betrayed. And on top of this, you have the extraordinary incompetence of the Department of Indian Affairs (which, I might remind you, is where our current prime minister began his ministerial career). It is entirely reasonable that Indians and their leadership should have developed a political rhetoric which puts *broken promises* in its centre. Today, of course, this rhetoric has been supplemented by another rhetoric, built around *rights*, but anyone who doubts the continuing relevance of the theme of *broken promises* should read *Drumbeat*, a collection of essays published by the Assembly of First Nations in 1989. The writers come back to it over and over again. Some of the essay titles make it clear enough: "The Mi'kmaq: The Covenant Chain" or "Algonquians South of the Ottawa: 220 Years of Broken Promises."[4] Both within Indian communities, and in the perceptions of the country as a whole, the Indian situation remains rooted in promises, and their breach.

This goes further, however. The total nature of Indians' victimization, the record of total failure to honour promises made to them, is highlighted by the total nature of the commitment those promises expressed. Indian treaties were taken by the Indians as a commitment to look after them and protect their welfare, in a total way. "The importance of the treaties," Harold Cardinal writes, "lies in the recognition and acceptance of the true spirit of the treaties." So, specific treaty provisions—the provision of farm implements, for example, or a medicine chest—are interpreted in the broadest fashion, as promises to insure the general welfare of Indian people. Cardinal, quoting a document from the Manitoba Indian Brotherhood, goes on: "A promise by the government and a carrying out of that promise to give economic and financial assistance to the Indian so that he may be better able to advance his economic position in the community would be a carrying out of the terms of the treaties. A promise and a carrying out of that promise that every child will have the right to a full education, is a carrying out of the terms of the treaties."[5] And so on. Moreover, this commitment is eternal; the treaties run *as long as the grass shall grow*. Suggestions by Mr. Trudeau and Mr. Chrétien in 1969 and 1970 that "treaties don't go on forever" (in fact, a reasonable view) have been called "infamous" by George Erasmus[6]—so far as Indians are concerned, they establish a continuing and unending relationship. Mr. Erasmus, though advancing a position of self-determination for Indians that borders on national sovereignty, will not give up the Indians' peculiar relationship to the federal government. "In our vision of a better Canada, the federal government would continue to act as a trustee, safeguarding the spirit and intent of the treaties . . ."[7]

In terms of promise, what this adds up to is clear enough: whatever the specific treaty provisions might have been, they invoked what I earlier called *the big promise*, the promise that lies behind all other promises—*I'll take care of it, I'll look after you*. Particular promises refer to some specific future, but the greater promise is of the future itself, stretching to eternity, or at least as far as a child can see. This was the promise made to the

Indians, as they see it, and it was broken. And this breach of trust was particularly felt because of the general ideological context in which it was made. That context was paternalism. Whether Indians "accepted" this paternalism, or had it imposed on them, is to a degree beside the point. The treaties and Indian interpretation of them were expressions of a Victorian view which saw the Indians as children, and proposed to "look after" them in those terms, and the anger that Indians feel today is expressed on that basis, whether they like to admit it or not (and of course they don't). Beyond all the particular broken promises, it is here, in the breach of this greater promise, that the true betrayal is found.

Now, again, we have to deal with a little history. The situation of Canadian Indians is defined by the treaties they've signed with the government (although many Indian groups, most significantly in British Columbia, Quebec and Labrador, never did sign any, or are only signing them now) but also by the Indian Act; and the Act, in many respects, is more important. The first Indian Act (using this name) was passed in 1876, but its antecedents go back to the pre-Confederation period. Defining Indian status and regulating Indians' civil rights and the administration of the reserves, its original intention was assimilationist in a fairly straightforward way. The cornerstone of this policy was "enfranchisement," which has a technical meaning within the Act, and involved a loss of Indian status, and the disabilities that went with that status, in exchange for the "full" rights of ordinary citizenship (including the vote, i.e., enfranchisement in the usual sense of the word). This process was envisioned as voluntary, a last step in Indian civil evolution. In fact, few Indians have ever taken "advantage" of it, and the largest group of enfranchised Indians consisted of Indian women, who automatically (and involuntarily) lost their Indian status when they married non-Indian men.

Over the years, the Act was revised several times, notably in 1951. By the late 1960s, however, it was clear to everyone that the Act was hopelessly out of date, indeed hopeless, period, and the new Trudeau government—with a young lad from Shawinigan, Jean Chrétien, heading up the Department of Indian Affairs—set about revising it. They held reasonably extensive consultations with Indian groups and leaders, who made it clear that they wanted their special status maintained, their traditional treaties honoured, and their various land claims settled. The "White Paper" issued by the government after these consultations and setting forth the government's proposals took a completely different tack. It downplayed questions associated with treaties and land claims, suggested the abolition of Indian status, and proposed to eventually eliminate the Department of Indian Affairs.

In effect, though working from different philosophical premises, the government's policy was actually a continuation of the former policy, represented by "enfranchisement." To be fair, though, the philosophical premises *were* different. The government accepted the folly of paternalism, while the extension to the Indian population of straightforward, full civil status was a clear rejection of the racist assumptions which had formerly defined relations between Indians and the government, and Indians and the wider society. The White Paper defined the *special status* of Indians as lying at the heart of their depressed social and economic situation: "the simple reality [is] that the separate legal status of Indians and the policies which flowed from it have kept the Indian people apart from and behind other Canadians."[8] Indians had been travelling on a "road of

Model Promises

different status, a road which has led to a blind alley of depriva-
tion and frustration. This road, because it is a separate road,
cannot lead to full participation, to equality in practice as well
as in theory."[9]

This view, liberal and humane, underlay the policy and its
recommendations. But Indians reacted with horror: the policy
was seen as "a thinly disguised programme of extermination
through assimilation."[10] They *wanted* their special status.
Regardless of its disabilities, their special status was clearly
defined by them as the core of their collective identity. Crudely,
it granted them numerous privileges, such as not paying taxes
under certain circumstances; besides, by this point, various court
cases and John Diefenbaker's unconditional extension of the
voting franchise to Indians (i.e., they didn't have to give up
Indian status to vote) had removed most of the actual legal
disabilities anyway. More importantly, Indians didn't want to
give up any of their treaty rights, nor any of their land claims (in
respect of those who had not signed treaties), nor lose their
special relationship with the federal government. Quickly, and
very skilfully, Indians organized against the White Paper. Making very effective use of the media, and public opinion—which
long since, and quite rightly, had moved to the Indians' side—
they attacked the White Paper with extraordinary ferocity. And,
astonishingly, in about eighteen months, the government backed
down.

I think you do have to say that this *was* astonishing; although
the White Paper, by definition, was a discussion paper, and not
hardened government policy, it's very rare for governments to
back away so completely from initiatives of this sort, especially
since this one had the personal support of the prime minister.

Above all, the government's retreat was testimony to the fierceness of the Indians' response; but other factors were also at work. The provinces were nervous: under the proposed policy, they would eventually have had to provide various services which the Indians had formerly received from the federal government. More cynically, Indian policy is never going to make or break a Canadian government, and Mr. Trudeau was a confident prime minister in the early years of his mandate: failure wasn't going to cost him too much. Less cynically—but just as truthfully—both Chrétien and Trudeau genuinely wanted to respond to a very real problem, and were reluctant to impose their views, given how opposed the Indians were.

But the failure of the White Paper created a quandary. Deliberately, the federal government had used the White Paper to raise the profile of the Indian question (anticipating a success), and the Indians' impassioned response had only heightened this. As well, the old Indian Act still needed revision; no one was happy with it. Moreover, it's hard not to believe that bureaucrats in the Department of Indian Affairs and the Secretary of State (which at this point still had a major role in Indian policy) and the Privy Council Office (which had actually drafted the White Paper) didn't see the failure of the White Paper as an opportunity. Bear in mind, the White Paper actually contemplated *disbanding* a huge government department, with a large budget and thousands of employees. As someone born and bred in Ottawa, let me assure you that this doesn't happen every day; come to think of it, I'm not sure it ever has—and it's not the sort of thing which federal bureaucrats take lying down. As it happens, my wife had started working for Indian Affairs only a few months before the White Paper was released. On the day it came out, she and other members of the staff were called together, given copies of the document, and addressed by a senior official. Afterwards, leaving the room, she remarked to an older colleague that it was just her luck—her first good job and it was dissolving under her. Her friend gave her the sort of look kindly gentlemen reserve for innocent girls and replied, "Don't worry. It will never happen." This was, of course, a sound view; and no doubt bureaucrats worked hard to see it prevailed. In any case, the solution developed couldn't have been a happier one from the point of view of Ottawa officialdom.

At the heart of this solution was *consultation*. Somewhat ingenuously, this was seen as a reason for the failure of the White Paper, although, by any reasonable definition, the government had actually consulted fairly broadly on it; it was just that they'd ignored most of what they'd heard. But clearly the traditional parliamentary definition of a consultative process—with White Papers, parliamentary committees and so forth—was inadequate to deal with this sort of problem. Moreover, by abandoning the White Paper and going back to square one, the government had created a real problem for itself. It was now committed to involving Indians much more intimately in policy formation. But which Indians, and how? Bureaucrats were now eager to have meetings with people—but who were they to meet with, and how were the agendas to be set? The problem was compounded by the extraordinarily complex and divided situation on the Indian side. Indians were "represented" by many groups, and many individual leaders—traditional leaders in the bands, the leadership of a variety of provincial organizations (such as the Saskatchewan Federation of Indians), a variety of other, more specialized organizations, and numerous prominent individuals of no particular affiliation. The trouble was, these groups and individuals were fractious to the extreme, and many had dubious legitimacy within their own communities. By 1970, as the failure of the White Paper became more and more obvious, the government and the bureaucracy desperately needed a credible "representative" of Indian people.

The solution to this problem was found in something called "The National Indian Brotherhood."

The NIB had first appeared on the scene in 1968, but it became especially important in 1970 when a group of men around Harold Cardinal (who'd come to prominence around his opposition to the White Paper) effectively took it over in a coup. And that is the only word. Through a remarkable series of manoeuvres, dependent on the failure of the NIB to legally register itself as a corporation with the Department of Consumer and Corporate Affairs, they effectively "refounded" the organization, and elected their own man, George Manuel, to its leadership. Over the next several years, Mr. Manuel was to prove himself a tremendously able and committed politician, but at the time he took over the NIB he faced enormous challenges. For one thing, it was far from being the most important Indian organization; for another, it was broke. His response was to fire half the staff (of four) and declare the organization bankrupt. This last decision was overruled by the NIB Executive Council, led by a group from Alberta (again, associated with Harold Cardinal). Taking advantage of the political situation around the White Paper, they instead lobbied the Privy Council Office and the Department of the Secretary of State to massively fund the organization. Those funds were, happily, forthcoming. Through the seventies, they fairly steadily increased; in fact, by 1979, the

Department of the Secretary of State, Indian Affairs, Health and
Welfare, CMHC and other government departments were
funding the NIB to the tune of perhaps two and a half million
dollars a year. These funds were applied to a variety of projects,
most self-evidently worthy, but the government was, of course,
paying for an organization which spent a good deal of time and
effort attacking it. This seems bizarre. But from the bureaucratic
point of view, it was not. No doubt some eyebrows were raised
when the NIB established relations with the government of
Libya, then as now a terrorist state, but the government and its
bureaucrats had what they wanted: a group that could be said to
"represent" Indians. The NIB was particularly useful because
it specifically claimed to represent status Indians (the Indians
covered under the Indian Act) and because it had attracted to
itself many young, dynamic Indian leaders. But, of course, the
government funded many other Indian and "native" organizations as well. It had to; it "*needs* these lobby groups to perform
for it what political scientists call 'demand aggregation' and
'interest articulation' functions. [It is] to a degree dependent on
Indian lobby groups to bring together, priorize, explain, and
suggest directions for the solution of problems."[11]

After this detour into history, we can now return to the
discourse of promise. And I'm sure the relevance of the Indian
example will be plain enough; it provided a general model for
organizing the government's relations to a host of "problems"
and interest groups associated with them. And that worked the
other way as well: it provided interest groups with a model that
allowed them to be taken seriously by government, receive funding from government, and have their "interests" placed on the
political agenda.

From the bureaucracy's point of view, what we have here is the philosopher's stone, the ultimate alchemist's spell. The lead of social problems is turned into the gold (yours, by the way) of "policy" and "program"—a heaven of jobs, offices, consultants, studies and reports. All that was needed was some group to declare itself aggrieved, some politician to make a promise—and the manna flowed, or fell, or whatever it does. And both interest groups and politicians were more than eager to play this game.

This model has three principal elements.

First, a *need* or *victimized* group must be identified and defined. It is obviously easier to do this if the need and victimization are objectively real—as is certainly the case with Canadian Indians—but that is scarcely necessary. The media, and the general political process, are crucial here. Concerted campaigns in the media, usually beginning with "human interest" features in newspapers and "special reports" on television, can quickly bring any "problem" into national prominence; and the normal dynamics of parliamentary politics can be counted on to keep the ball rolling.

Secondly, the problem must have *representation*. Problems cannot exist abstractly. They must be embodied in organizations and leaders. Such organizations must have some claim to a constitutional, representative character, though this can be more or less notional. The NIB, for example, simply made every status Indian an ex officio member of its organization whether people wished to be or not. This representative character is then legitimized by the bureaucracy, and any administrative difficulties can be taken care of by government funding. At the present time, there can be few Canadians who are not "represented" in this fashion.

Thirdly, directly, the discourse of promise comes into play at the political level: political leaders make *promises* to the relevant organizations and leaders to "deal with" their "problem," as it has now been defined and legitimized.

Rooted in the particular history of Canadian Indians, and feeding off it, the generality of this model can't be doubted. Indeed, it is now a standard part of government, summarized dryly in a standard textbook on Canadian political science:

> At the policy-initiation stage, we see the bureaucracy act-ing both as a channel of input and as a *gatekeeper* in filter-ing demands from the environment, and as an *advocate* for interests of specific clientele. In the advocacy role, the govern-ment department enters into a sort of symbiotic relationship with the relevant interest groups in jointly attempting to con-vince the priority setters in the Cabinet and the central agen-cies to meet the policy demands of their shared clientele. The interest group–departmental relationship is symbiotic because a successful campaign that influences the priority setters to embrace the desired policy or program benefits both the department and interest group. The latter benefits directly in that the clientele group it represents gets an immediate payoff from the new program. The former benefits through the increased budget and human resources it gets to implement the new policy.[12]

Despite this generality, however, we mustn't lose sight of its particular origins. For even though there may have been other sources, there's no doubt that the history of the Canadian Indian has left a peculiar and indelible mark upon this development.

All social "problems" lie in the shadow of this one. Most especially, we must bear in mind the very specific political context of those origins—the rejection of the White Paper. Whatever its defects, the White Paper set forth a response to the situation of the Canadian Indian that was rooted in fundamental notions of citizenship: equality before the law, equal treatment by government and dignified and full participation in a common civil life—*special status* for no one.

This was rejected.

That rejection was legitimized by government and broadly accepted in society.

And so, from that point forward, the question of government, increasingly, was who had special status, and how was it defined; the principal business of politics became that definition.

For a time, after it was published, Mr. Trudeau and his government attempted to defend the White Paper. In a speech in Vancouver—frequently cited with contempt by Indians—Mr. Trudeau said: "We can go on treating the Indians as having a special status. We can go on adding bricks of discrimination around the ghetto in which they live and at the same time perhaps helping them preserve certain cultural traits and certain ancestral rights. Or we can say you're at a crossroads—the time is now to decide whether the Indians will be a race apart in Canada or whether it will be Canadians of full status [*sic*]. And this is a difficult choice . . . *It's inconceivable, I think, that in a given society one section of the society have a treaty with the other section of the society. We must all be equal under the law and we must not sign treaties amongst ourselves.*"[13] This defence failed. The discourse of promises, by definition, implies special status, *ad infinitum*, and—precisely—the total division of society by treaties, *promises*, amongst ourselves. Today, we may not all be Indians, but we all belong to different tribes.

Promises, Promises

In summary, we can see how *promise* has been developed and legitimized in particular Canadian ways. All the elements in the Canadian model—federal-provincial relations, hinterland politics, Indians—support, and then exploit, a discourse of division and incoherence. Within this, society, as a whole, has vanished; party programs have given way to incoherent, contradictory lists of promises targeted to groups, regions, sexes, ages—the list of victimized and needy tribes by now is endless. This is a closed system, characterized by its egoism—*more, more, more*—and its irresponsibility, particularly to realistic constraint: a system exemplified by the surreal world of federal-provincial relations. In those relations, we can see the aspects of *promise* that are especially dependent on childhood, just as its irrational, emotional and apocalyptic side is mirrored in our hinterland politics. Of course, this is only a matter of emphasis; all the aspects of *promise* exist in each of these models, to varying degrees. That is partly the reason for its triumph; *promise* is all pervasive, legitimated by some of the most important developments in the country's history, and now thoroughly saturating our political life. Inevitably, we are not alone. The problems of conducting politics in complex, massified, heterogeneous societies have meant that political discourse in other western countries somewhat resembles our own. But our particular history has stamped *promise* with a peculiar Canadian accent. Dividing us, keeping us apart, it's a game we've all learned to play together, in our special way. Ironic—as the sportscasters say.

Chapter Four

—◦—

The Big Promise

*T*oday, the discourse of promise dominates politics in every way—political advertising, the talk of the politicians themselves, the whole world of political commentary. In Ontario, political junk mail fills our letter boxes: *The Harris government promised to restore jobs, hope, growth and opportunity. We are delivering.* Really—hope? opportunity? Well done! On the other hand, a man in British Columbia is suing the premier, Glen Clark, for breaking his election promises and uttering an assortment of untruths—and though he won't win his case, he should. And journalists, of course, scribble away: Anthony Wilson-Smith (*Maclean's*, "Backstage Ottawa"): *Promises and pain . . .*[1] David Frum (*Financial Post*, "What's Right"): *One gets the impression the leader is delivering promises with his fingers crossed behind his back.*[2] William Pfaff (*International Herald Tribune*): *Whichever of the parties wins the British National Election on May 1, the question has to be asked, win for what? This is a campaign with few serious promises made, and without a vision . . .*[3] This is so common that no one notices; it's the forest we never see for the trees.

But the ubiquity and insistence of *promise* not only reflect its triumph; they also testify to a crisis—a crisis of faith, belief, trust.

It's a crisis that goes far beyond the breach of any particular promise, such as the GST, or the mendacity of any particular politician, whether Glen Clark or Chrétien or Bouchard. And it's not just a Canadian crisis; throughout the western world there's a pervasive sense of anxiety, unease, failure. Its most obvious cause is the slump of the early nineties, the most complete economic collapse of western capitalism since the Great Depression. That slump didn't just destroy incomes; it undermined the fundamental assumption of western politics since the Second World War—economic growth, the ever-expanding economic pie. This growth, and the relative social justice it created, played the decisive role in resisting Soviet totalitarianism, generating the pressure that ended the Cold War. But even as the economies of Europe recover from that slump, they are still left with unemployment rates around the same level as Canada's, a situation unheard of in the sixties and seventies. Moreover, the collapse wasn't only economic; it also represented an *intellectual* reversal. It marked the end of Keynesianism, at least as practised by western governments; and since the crisis came, in many countries, after long periods of social democratic rule—and was probably worst in Scandinavia, the promised land of social democracy—it exposed the intellectual bankruptcy of the democratic left. Accordingly, free markets and "privatization" have carried the day in both theory and practice, redefining politics both in Europe and North America. Reagan's greatest triumph is Clinton, the "new" democrat; Margaret Thatcher's most satisfactory achievement, at least to herself, must surely be Tony Blair; and every time Paul Martin brings down a budget, Michael Wilson gives a nod and says "told you so." Still, despite all this, it's people, ordinary people, who've been affected most of all.

Their morale has been shattered. Optimism is dead. People are afraid—that they'll lose their jobs, won't get their pensions; and are even *irrationally* afraid—people believe in UFOs again, see pedophiles and rapists everywhere. Worse yet: the young seem to be most frightened of all.

In relation to *promise*, this malaise takes a specific form, finds a characteristic expression—we've lost our faith in "the big promise," the general promise that lies behind all the little ones.

Society, represented by the government, will *look after us*. Society, represented by the government, will make sure *everything's all right.*

Since the sixties, faith in this "big promise" has been the basic assumption of people's lives. Life—from school to retirement— was assured. In the nineties, that assurance has been destroyed. Of course, we still *want* it. We still think it's our *right*. So our loss of faith produces frustration, anger, resentment. We *blame*— Mulroney or Chrétien or "big business" or "big government" or the decline of religion or men or sexual promiscuity or "baby boomers" or the Americans . . . The particular targets are selected by prejudice, and like all such are inherently irrational, but that doesn't make any difference; we're not trying to solve anything, just release our rage.

The loss of faith in "the big promise" marks the most important change in political attitudes in a generation.

Its most obvious manifestation, not surprisingly, is our extraordinary sensitivity to *promise* itself. Having lost faith in the "big promise," our sensitivity around each particular promise has been incredibly heightened; we don't let the poor bastards get away with anything now. And, while we believe all the more strongly in *promise*, we feel an increasing frustration with it: like rats in a maze, we run faster and faster, but feel more and more trapped. Accordingly, anxiety, frustration and anger define the contours of the contemporary political map.

Promise, with its tendency to encourage and legitimize the fragmentation—virtual atomization—of the electorate fits right in. Breaking the electorate down into particular "targets" not only destroys the idea (and reality) of a common citizenship, it also destroys social solidarity. Since we no longer exist as Canadians, but only subsets—Chinese Canadians, western Canadians, gay Canadians—we feel ourselves divided, diminished and increasingly vulnerable. Deprived of ties to our actual nationality, we are reduced to connections, largely ephemeral, to ideological constructs ("sisterhood"). But our response—the response of *promise*—is to intensify this. With the economic pie no longer expanding, the only way for my piece to grow bigger is for yours to shrink. Accordingly, everyone is anxiously seeking some sort of leverage, and *promise* offers the rhetoric and political mechanism to achieve this. Hilariously—so it must seem to them—everyone now demands Indian status, a position of privileged victimization. No doubt, in an attempt to maintain middle-class standards (i.e., pay the mortgage) women have been most successful at this, but in fact it's now the universal social strategy. Indeed, the triumph of *promise* is so complete that no other strategy is *thinkable*, for ideology, as traditionally understood, has virtually disappeared. "Left" and "Right" are no longer connected to the political and philosophical tendencies that previously defined them. Canadian conservatives, for example, have long since abandoned the tradition that includes, say, John Macdonald, R.B. Bennett, and George Grant; and to label the "politically correct" left as Stalinist only

92

bewilders it, for its adherents are utterly disassociated from the history with which they pretend to identify. As a practical matter, virtually every Canadian political actor is some sort of liberal, and terms like *left* and *right* merely refer to different styles: on the "left," a crude, moralizing militancy; on the right, a truculent, moralistic individualism. You will note the common term. But in the discourse of promise, the available intellectual framework, even if it's not explicitly called upon, is essentially religious. And the principal motivation is less connected with objective, social reality than an interior, subjective condition, an egoism which moralism satisfies: the absolute insistence that, yes, I am a good little girl or boy, and therefore deserving. Indeed, since analytical and programmatic thinking virtually disappear within the discourse of promise, moralizing actually becomes the principal, even sole, political activity of most polit- ical actors; analyzing problems, or thinking up solutions to them, gives way completely to the strenuous assertion of right- eousness. *Promise*, in effect, has scooped out the content of political ideas, transforming them into signs, whose meaning is wholly emotional and—significantly—largely nostalgic. There are no new ideas. Instead, "the left" pretends to "defend" an ide- alized past of "social programs" and "government involvement," while the right attempts to reinstate a Christian utopia of upright, moral individualism. In fact, both are appealing to a yearning for the "big promise," which exists as a fantasized past and a subjective state, the security of the child who believes *everything will be all right.*

Two concrete examples illustrate both how completely "the big promise" has been forsaken, and how people attempt to cope with it.

I

My first example allows me to indulge in a little nostalgia myself. I originally became involved in Canadian politics through the peace movement—Bomarc and Bertrand Russell, strontium-90 and Kay Macpherson—and one of the friends I retain from those days is Ken Drushka. He lives now in B.C., writing books on west-coast subjects while being raised by his children, but occasionally he comes through town and we drink. As it happens, we worked together during the sixties, but I'd actually heard of Ken before then; he was the editor of *The Varsity*, the U of T student newspaper, and he wrote an editorial calling for the abolition of Remembrance Day on the grounds that it was a glorification of war. This must have been in 1962 or 1963—conceivably I was still in high school (Ken, agreeably enough, is somewhat older than I am). In any case, in those days, this sort of suggestion was bound to cause a furor, and I remember it being reported as a major item on the CBC radio news, which is where I heard it. I was astonished—not at the furore, but the suggestion. It had never occurred to me that Remembrance Day glorified war; surely the contrary. How could anyone see Ypres as attractive? I'd always bought a poppy in the fall, continued to wear one during my ban-the-bomb days, and indeed do so still. Moreover, despite my objections to western and Canadian defence policy, it never occurred to me to despise the military or military men, nor did I see any contradiction between my politics and an appreciation for Canadian military history (which is tremendously important and interesting).

When I eventually met Ken, we argued mildly about this, and though I wouldn't want to put words into either of our mouths after so long, I remember something about Remembrance Day just being for "old vets boozing it up at the Legion." And probably there's something in that. All the same, it's aston- The Big ishing how much Canadian social legislation—and "progressive" Promise legislation generally—first developed around veterans and the wars they fought in. The first Canadian women granted the franchise were relatives of members of the armed forces; the first Indians to vote were servicemen in World War I. And Canada's first large-scale experience with social programs, as we would now understand the term, came around the veterans of the world wars.

The reason, of course, is that veterans were the first Canadians to attract a general, national sense of obligation, and their circumstances were clearly the result of government policy: responsibility—political and moral—was clear.

As usual in our history, the First World War was the most important. About 650,000 men and women served in Canadian or Allied armies, out of a total population of 8 million; in fact one-third of Canadian men of military age eventually put on uniform; almost half a million went overseas; more than 60,000 never came back; and of those who did return, something like 70,000 suffered serious disabilities.

In other words, the Great War—on top of everything else—created a social problem. Fascinatingly, the differing aspects of that problem still define Canadian social policy, because it was a health problem, an income problem and a problem of social integration.

It was a health problem, because by far the greatest number of men invalided out of the military were suffering from diseases rather than combat wounds—there was a great demand for prostheses, but even more for hospital care; it was an income problem because of the need and demand for pensions—aside from the veterans themselves, the war created more than thirty thousand widows and orphans; and it was a problem of social integration on many fronts, but most importantly job training.

Most of the arguments around these issues still have a very familiar ring. The government was terribly afraid of the overall cost—stern cries of fiscal responsibility were heard in the land. But then they had to watch their own pension expenditures rise from $70,000 in 1912 to $7 million in 1918 to $25 million by the end of 1920—at which point, 177,000 men, women and children were receiving some kind of benefit.[4][*] There was, of course, tremendous anxiety about cheating—tales of deathbed marriages by crafty ladies who turned themselves into instant widows—and a truly righteous fear that too high a level of benefits might discourage initiative: "Everyone must understand," wrote John L. Todd, a designer of the system, "that armless, legless men *can* become self-supporting";[5] I'm sure contemporary proponents of "workfare" would be the first to agree. And since we're dealing with money and politicians in Canada, you would naturally expect constitutional disputes; job training, as per usual, was a major issue, though the problem province wasn't Quebec, but Ontario.

Ultimately, a reasonably good system—in many respects better than those of the other Allied nations—was put together, but of course it incurred criticism. Some of this came from vets themselves, who began to form organizations, which ultimately

* They were also acutely aware that in the U.S., even before the Great War, about 20 per cent of government expenditures went toward pensions and related military benefits. This was referred to as "The Pension Evil."

led to the Canadian Legion—the first major advocacy group in the country. (Interestingly, there was an appreciation of the dangers here—of soldiers "banded together in Associations, serving their particular interests, as distinguished from those of the Nation."[6]) One of the major criticisms coming from the vets was democratically inspired: pensions, especially for the totally disabled, should be made equal as between officers and men. And complaints from other quarters also marked a gathering shift in philosophy, away from philanthropy and élitism toward values that echo the language, especially the "universalism," of social programs today. For example, a committee of concern— a bishop, archdeacon, president of U of T—urged the case for a government veterans' program this way:

> For twenty, thirty, forty and, in some cases, even fifty years, support must be given, and it must be drawn from a source absolutely stable and secure. We owe our defenders no less than this. We must save them from both the humiliation and uncertainty of public charity, and give them permanent and adequate *security* from want, paid them not as a favour but *as a right*, for it would be an unpardonable insult to a body of brave men if the payment of a pension carried with it the faintest trace of charity or the least suspicion of patronage.[7]

Politicians quickly picked up on this. From the beginning, parliamentary discussion of veterans' questions had been entirely nonpartisan; Borden would move motions, Laurier would second them. The Special Parliamentary Committee of 1916 "was a model of nonpartisan zeal"—any opposition member with an interest in its proceedings was invited to join. Almost inevitably, this universal, nonpartisan spirit—which saw, in veterans, just another aspect of the national interest—infiltrated both the language and substance of the measures taken on their behalf. When the Unionist government was formed (Borden's Conservatives, plus pro-conscription Liberals), their manifesto referred to the vets this way: "Duty and decency demand that those who are saving democracy shall not find democracy a house of privilege, or a school of poverty and hardship."[8] As a general philosophy, this was sufficiently egalitarian to smack (at the time) of socialism; but in relation to the vets, it was merely a platitude. By the time the reforms of the Ralston Commission were implemented, there was "a hint, albeit faint, of a future in which all citizens, not merely veterans, might share entitlement, not charity."[9]

But before this happy denouement, there was to be a second, tragic act. The experience of the First World War had been sufficiently difficult that the government, almost as soon as the Second World War broke out, was putting plans in place to deal with a new generation of vets: in December, 1939—not three months after Canada had declared war—a special committee of cabinet was formed "to consider the problems arising from the demobilization of members of the Armed Forces." And throughout the war "able and dedicated men, most of them veterans themselves, of all political persuasions and from almost every field of the country's life, produced a stream of recommendations which resulted in government action."[10] Note, again, the non-partisanship. And it was in this spirit that the legislation produced was labelled "The Veterans Charter"—*a big promise*, a pledge, a covenant, that came from the country as a whole, rather than a particular party or government.

The Charter provided a potpourri of benefits, from a clothing allowance to land grants, but the most important again concerned pensions, health and retraining.

Pensions, as the minister of veterans affairs put it in 1971, formed "the cornerstone of the Charter."[11] After the First World War, they had been ground-breaking, for it was the country's first large-scale experience with providing them; but the Old Age Pension had been established in 1927,[†] so that the novelty of veterans' pensions after the Second World War was established around their administration and questions such as "means tests." The situation regarding health benefits was different, however. These were very comprehensive (they included complete dental rehabilitation) and were a clear forerunner to all other government health schemes that have followed. Injured veterans were to receive free care as long as they lived, and the disabled were to be rehabilitated as far as possible; moreover, all vets received free medical care for a year after their discharge. The scope of this was enormous; by 1946, the Department of Veterans Affairs was running thirty-six hospitals and treatment centres across the country (some very large) and had about 25,000 in-patients—a fair share of the health delivery system at the time.

Even more innovative were provisions for training and education. These included all kinds of vocational training as well as university, and covered everything from tuition and textbooks to various living allowances and loans. Again, the scale was enormous. Vets, taking advantage of their university benefits, more than doubled the university population in 1945. Whole

† The first public pension was actually a Mother's Pension in B.C. in 1920.

institutions were created—for example, the Training and Re-establishment Institute of Toronto (which later became Ryerson). Including vets from Korea, some 85,000 received vocational training, and more than 35,000 graduated from university. This wasn't "free" education; but it enormously democratized Canadian education, especially at the university level.

Taken together, all these programs—the whole history, running back to the Great War—have obviously played a crucial role in the development of Canadian social policy. The vets, in effect, became exemplary, ideal Canadians. They had sacrificed themselves—or been prepared to sacrifice themselves—for the country as a whole. They could be treated, therefore, in an ideal way. But of course that ideal gradually became generalized; the debt the country owed the vets also began to define the debt owed to all citizens, what they began to assume the country could give.

Here, of course, you have the relation to *promise*, and the "big promise" especially. And this is why I think the first major breach of the promise made to the vets has a particular interest. This came in Michael Wilson's budget of February, 1990, when the government decided to save $17 million by changing the board and lodging charges for vets in chronic-care facilities: in effect, a claw-back, effectively reducing their pensions by more than 20 per cent. This was, in the words of the Canadian Legion, "the first abrupt budget cancellation of a benefit for veterans without warning or substitution."[12] But here's the most interesting point of all; *no one noticed*. The *Globe* reported the changes as part of its regular budget coverage, but there was no editorial—nor any letters-to-the-editor in the following weeks. A few papers did give it some play, but the only national commentary was a piece in *The Financial Post*, by Duncan

Cameron. Otherwise, silence . . . and like the dog that didn't bark in the Sherlock Holmes story, I think this silence is significant.

It testifies, obviously, to the declining political importance of Canadian vets. There are fewer of them; their status has been eroded by years of belittling Canada's military history—and their own absurd antics about the flag, people wearing turbans in their bars and so forth. All the same, there are still a lot of vets, and the Legion remains a significant organization—there's no way to marginalize vets; but they're now only one group among many. And that's the point. In the same budget that cut the benefits for vets, there were cuts to women's groups, which incited the most fulsome wrath. But why should someone like Judy Rebick, say, care about the vets—they're not *her* group, not her people. The vets once stood up for the nation, but when Wilson brought his budget down, there was no longer a nation to stand up for them: or at least that would be the sentimental way of putting it. In fact, the nation was still there; but its political discourse no longer had room for its expression.

Ironically, this can all be seen easily enough in one of the surprise defenders of the Wilson budget: Doug Fisher. Writing in *The Legion*, where he has a regular column, he declared the cuts to be "reasonable," especially in light of "the large annual deficits Ottawa's had for 16 straight years."[13] This provoked a storm of angry letters, which Mr. Fisher used as the basis of a subsequent column. "When the country called for help," wrote one of his correspondents, "those who are now veterans responded without stint and proudly supplied the only volunteer force in the major powers." Another simply said: "This is not the Canada veterans fought and died for." I would say he's right, and Mr. Fisher I think backs me up when he says:

There are several points of explanation, rather than defence, that I want to make. Firstly, there are presently 6,800 Canadians living who served in WW I and just over half a million who served in WW II. In general terms, a large proportion of citizens volunteered in both wars. Take WW II: about one million volunteered, 900,000 of them male. The total population at the time was between 11 and 12 million. It's staggering when you consider that the million came from less than four million who were of an age to be useful in the forces. That's why I think those of us who volunteered and served, including myself and my friends, many of whom did not return, as not having done anything exceptional during the Canada of that time. We were part of a country at war . . . This concept I have has underpinned my belief that veterans are part of the whole.[14]

But that concept is scarcely tenable today. The whole has been split into too many parts, and our political discourse now works with this as a fundamental assumption. "The big promise," as I've been talking about it, may strike some people as just another term for *the social contract*; but the social contract assumes a society with some integrity and unity, especially at the level of values—and from that unity can evolve (as it did around veterans and their affairs) notions and structures like *the welfare state*. But *promise*, even when it's demanding "benefits" from government, and may even be identifying with these older notions, functions quite differently. That's why the relations between the vets and society, conceived in those older terms, was vulnerable—the dog didn't bark in the night because it was dead.

Still, sometimes even silence is resonant. Wilson's various cuts at "the social safety net" could succeed because the nation that had put that net together had disappeared; the old definition of citizenship, which is clearly still real to Doug Fisher, has vanished. Government programs, the results of all those promises made to all those "interest" groups to deal with all those "issues" as defined by the CBC, are no longer a response to, or justified in terms of, national priorities or values. And so the programs, in the end, can only be defended by the particular groups that benefit from them. One by one, through the late eighties and nineties, those promises have been broken or reneged on; and just as children learn to be confident about the world through promises *kept*, so we've come to lose faith and confidence because of promises *broken*. The attack on the vets highlights how profoundly our faith in *the big promise* has been undermined. But it's important to understand that this isn't because Michael Wilson was a "bad" man, or even a "right-wing" man— the budgetary problems he faced were genuine enough. The real problem was the political discourse that had created those promises and programs in the first place.

II

The vets had pretty much finished with Ryerson in 1948, and my friend Ken Drushka actually attended it during the early sixties, before moving on to U of T. Now we'll skip ahead thirty years. Because, oddly, some of my present-day young friends are also Ryerson graduates and their situation, in a certain awful sense, is exemplary.

One of them is a young woman, whose name is Gertrude— which, as I keep telling her, is a wonderful, old-fashioned name. She shouldn't worry about it anyway; she's gorgeous, her head is stuffed full of brains, and she's as up-to-date as an Avid editing machine. Film, in fact, is her passion. Ryerson now has an excellent film school—both on the "creative" and technical sides—and Gertrude emerged from it full of honours and passion and energy, and some $23,000 dollars in debt—her student loans. I was staggered when she told me this figure, because I knew, throughout her school career, that she'd been getting some help from home, had often worked as a waitress and lived the usual wretched student existence. Besides, through her, I met another graduate, a young man named Pieter—who, on completion of his education, found himself in the hole by something over $30,000, a staggering burden for a man in his early twenties. And these debts, mind you, are not owed to indulgent relatives or understanding bureaucrats. They're bank loans: six months after they graduated, both received letters from the CIBC setting out the terms on which they were expected to pay them off. Gertrude is still struggling. Pieter did his level best—and then, after losing a job, declared personal bankruptcy . . . which makes a really great start to life.

These cases are far from exceptional. More than 40 per cent of university graduates—and the percentage is rising—leave school in debt: in the early eighties, by something over $5,000, today by $17,000, and projected figures see this figure rising to well over $20,000 by the end of the decade. In Ontario, the number of recipients of the provincial assistance program jumped 50 per cent between 1991 and 1995, the size of the average loan doubling as well. At York University in Toronto, student debt loads doubled in five years to just under $10,000. At the University College of Cape Breton, more than 80 per cent require government assistance to finance their education.

For students, the consequences are inevitable—and often disastrous. From 1990 to 1996, students declaring bankruptcy more than doubled; indeed, so many students were declaring personal bankruptcy as a result of their student loans that in 1996 the federal government introduced legislation to make it more difficult.‡ All this is coming at a time when unemployment among students and recent college graduates is very high. Unemployment for young people between the ages of 15 and 24 has been twice the rate for older Canadians (25–54) throughout the past decade. For graduating students, the outlook is bleak—we all know the stories about taxi drivers with Master's degrees. But these aren't just stories. Even by late 1996—after several years of economic expansion—the unemployment rate for young university graduates was over 10 per cent, and if one excludes those working at jobs unrelated to their education, the rate is very much higher.[15] Their income situation is not exactly thrilling, either. In 1993, recent graduates who *could* find jobs earned about the same, in real terms, as a high-school graduate in the 1970s.[16]

I won't belabour these statistics; everyone knows that this is a difficult time to be entering the work force, and everyone knows, at least in a vague way, that a university education isn't "worth what it used to be." But I think we can overlook how significant this is, how much this realization undercuts the

‡ Yes, some students are cheats and use personal bankruptcy as a way of avoiding their loans; but don't kid yourself—most personal bankrupts, including student bankrupts, are desperate. The government, in effect, recognized this the next year when they introduced further legislation extending interest relief on student loans to thirty months. The amount of legislation in the nineties testifies to the disarray of policy in the whole area.

world we think we have made. The basis for all politics in Western democracies since the Second World War was an expanding economic pie, and the way that people claimed their slice of the pie was education—and especially university education. Since 1945, the Bachelor of Arts degree has been the guarantee of prosperity in Canada and everywhere else. And not just prosperity. University education was a mark of status—middle-class status—and a general acceptance of mainstream, modern values. Moreover, for the generation that lived through the Depression, university graduation became the ultimate way of dealing with the tremendous sense of economic insecurity which that catastrophe left behind. With a university degree in hand, *everything would be all right.* Nothing has expressed and embodied "the big promise" more than university education. Nothing has undermined it more than the collapse of our faith in the university system. And it's hard to imagine a bigger breach of *promise* than the current situation facing university students. They emerge from university burdened with debts and with poor job prospects. For the parents of today's graduates, a university degree gave them tickets to the best seats in the house; today's graduates are standing behind a pillar fifty rows from the stage. They are, of course, demoralized. But that demoralization has seeped out, and pervades the whole of society. We all know that if a university degree can't guarantee the future, then no such guarantee exists.

What's happened here?

First, we have to understand why today's students end up so deep in the hole. At the heart of this is the peculiar nature of the financial assistance available to Canadian students, a system that pushes them, inevitably, into debt. *Canada is one of the few major countries with no national system of student grants.* Whereas the United States, Australia and most European countries have large programs to give deserving students unconditional grants to advance their education, Canada only provides assistance through loans.§ More and more students have been requiring those loans—about half of students have them today—and the loans get bigger and bigger; in 1992–93, more than half the students eligible for loans were assessed as needing more than $6,000 *for that year alone* and 17 per cent required more than $10,000. These needs have been accelerating, no doubt, because the difficult economic times of recent years have made summer and part-time jobs harder to come by; but the more fundamental reason is that university education is becoming more and more expensive. Why? Largely because of *tuition fees*. In 1980, about 13 per cent of university general operating income came from tuition fees; by 1995–96, this figure had grown to almost 30 per cent. In the 1993–94 year, students paid a total of $2 billion dollars in tuition. And of course a huge percentage of that $2 billion was borrowed money. But these increases and vast outlays are not a reflection of greedy universities but rather of their own hard necessity—the result of cuts to education by both the federal and various provincial governments. In Alberta, for example, the government has cut funding to education by 21 per cent. But the problem is hardly isolated. In just five years, across the country, total government support for university operating budgets has dropped from 80 per cent to 70 per cent, and that trend will continue. Although the actual effects vary from university to university, the general conclusion—advanced by

The Big Promise

§ Some provinces, notably Quebec, do have limited grant programs and there are a few specialized grants at the federal level, i.e., for female doctoral students.

the Association of Universities and Colleges—is inescapable: "In fact, with recent increases in tuition fees, fees now cover well over a third of the operating costs in many institutions. Universities are increasingly publicly-assisted rather than publicly-funded institutions." In other words, our universities are well on the way to "privatization"—and it's the students who are paying.

Now, there are many arguments around these issues, but for the moment I want to ignore them and consider this in terms of *promise*. First—I don't think you can emphasize this too strongly—university education was one of the chief institutional supports for "the big promise"; its failure has more than a particular, local importance—it undermines our fundamental confidence in our social system; it constitutes a major breach of trust, which reverberates well beyond the university itself. No doubt that is particularly true because university education involves young people, promises between generations.

But just because the university has been so important, the current situation is truly extraordinary. And of course that's the point, or part of it; the university today is simply not as important as it used to be. The withdrawal of governments from university funding and the decline in the economic utility of the university degree both point toward a *general decline* in the status of the university; we don't value it as much as we once did. That's the reason governments have been able to pull back from funding postsecondary education without paying much of a political price, and why the plight of Canadian students hasn't reverberated much more loudly than that of the vets.

How has this happened?

A generation ago, the universities were at the centre of political agendas; a generation ago, university values, culture and training were central to the kind of society we wanted to create. Now, a truly dreadful situation is building within our universities and Canadian student life, but no one cares or notices. Why?

Once again, I think *promise* is a major part of the answer.

I've been taking much of my information about the plight of today's universities from a document called *Strategy for Change*, written by Denise Doherty-Delorme and "the staff collective" of the Canadian Federation of Students. This is a detailed, thorough and well-reasoned exposition of the situation I've only sketched. And just to be absolutely clear, I think the situation Ms. Delorme has described is a national disgrace. Nonetheless, as I read through her document, I found it easier and easier to understand why governments have been able to get away with underfunding our universities and bankrupting our students, and why, with scarcely a murmur, universities are now ceasing to represent a public trust and are quickly falling into private hands. Ms. Delorme doesn't care very much about our universities either.

Indeed, what's extraordinary about this document, in some ways so excellent, is that it doesn't betray even the slightest interest in education. Why is education important? Ms. Delorme advances and accepts, even though she doesn't enthusiastically advocate, an economist view of the university's value—it encourages economic growth, enhances productivity. Briefly, in a quotation, she genuflects toward the "noneconomic benefits" such as "literary and cultural values" which the university provides, but her most positive statement is a mishmash of banalities about coming to terms with technological change and conflicting social values. The university, she happily concludes, serves democratic ideals: "we must strive to give all Canadians the education required to make sophisticated judgements about the future of our country."[17] In other words, the university is a tool valuable for social mobility and social integration.

Indeed, her critique of the current system is put entirely in those terms. Almost all her complaints (which are completely valid) ultimately become concerns about accessibility—denying university education to young people who can't afford it. And this is a tremendously important problem. But how is accessibility defined? "Access to postsecondary education is defined as the removal of barriers to ensure the right of entry of all students who are able and willing to study, to learn, regardless of socio-economic background and/or place of residence."[18]

Note the rather convoluted expression here. But it's necessary, because Ms. Delorme is hoping you'll think she's saying something which she isn't. She hopes that you'll imagine she's saying something like, Every *deserving* student should have a place in university, or, The university should be open to everyone who *shows they can benefit from it*. Actually, she's saying something quite different—that anyone should have the right to go to university, no matter what. That little phrase, *who are able and willing to study, to learn,* doesn't actually mean that university entrants should *know* anything. "Know" would imply standards, and standards must (a) be rationalized and (b) discriminate. And that is anathema. Because what we're really talking about here is the fulfilment of a promise—*and every child shall have the right to a university education*—and promises, as we have seen, are emotional, not rational, and must be unconditional.

Here, in its entirety, is the very first paragraph of Ms. Delorme's section on "The Goal of Post-Secondary Education":

In 1836, the Legislative Council of Upper Canada, appointed by the British Crown, vetoed a motion which proposed that every child had the right to attend school. The group thought only the "*sons*" of the "*establishment*" should receive any schooling as they would be the ones eventually running the country. Very few *public funds* were allocated to the *public schools.*[19]

Remember, this paragraph begins and frames a discussion of the *goals* of postsecondary education; but right away those become goals of social mobility and integration—there's not the slightest interest in *what* might be taught students, and why.

But of course this paragraph is completely consistent with *promise*. Immediately, the problem is seen in terms of interest groups, and a victim is implicitly sought—though it couldn't be more ridiculous in this case, because "daughters"—young women—have been a slight majority of university enrolment for years, and even though the class background in universities is narrowing, contemporary enrolments are scarcely confined to members of the establishment.

Ms. Delorme continues as she begins; there's no concern with the intellectual content of education, with excellence, and no mention of standards, or rigour, or work. Again, that's entirely consistent with *promise*. Promises are accepted, granted, received; you ask and hope, and they're given. You don't *work* for them. Promises are about faith. Promises are about who you are, not what you do. This is why, as her critique continues, there's never a question of *merit*. Merit—standards—qualifications: these constitute a kind of quibbling which *promise* always finds suspect. Moreover, they are rational; they assume and imply a totally different kind of discourse. And the potential outcomes are insupportable—engineering classes, for example, conceivably filled with nothing but boys.

But all this merely reflects well-established academic trends— the university in which Ms. Delorme herself was educated. No one there seriously disagrees with her. The content of education has long since been subordinated to a peculiar fundamentalist egalitarianism, whose Protestantism, interestingly enough, was a hallmark of the Legislative Council to which Ms. Delorme so objects. Today's university justifies itself in terms of a crude economism and as a vehicle for social integration. Educational, intellectual and pedagogical content is displaced to the periphery.

This, undoubtedly, is a change. Of course it's easy enough to romanticize the university of the past, to allow its trailing ivy to obscure its élitism, or to hear nothing but the echoes of Shakespeare and Milton in its hallowed halls. But that's not necessary; whatever the "classical" university may actually have been, it's true to say that during the fifties and sixties the university, in addition to the traditional professional training which it offered, could appeal to society for support on at least three grounds:

1. The university had a legitimate call upon our High Culture. The university insisted on the importance of that High Culture, defining itself as a place where it was studied and practised—and society, however hypocritically, still deemed this worthy of support.

2. The university was the home (the originator, as a practical matter) of the new social, economic and statistical sciences that were crucial to the rise of social programs, social engineering and macro-economics in government—and to the burgeoning new advertising and communications industries that were exploding at that time. In fact, government and

advertising were the defining industries of the period 1950–1970, and the university, especially its social sciences, was crucial to both.

3. Lastly, the university provided a source of expertise and understanding—from area studies to psychology—that was directly tied to the Cold War. The university (and this includes the Canadian university) was an integral and valuable part of the Cold War state.

All of this has changed.

The university no longer defines itself in terms of the traditional High Culture, and doesn't even seriously pretend to study it—the faculty doesn't want to teach it, the students probably don't want to learn it. So the curriculum which defined the university for centuries has now been marginalized. Those older disciplines have been replaced by all the "studies"—of media, culture, women and so on. But—as a way of justifying support—these simply do not have the *cachet* of the older, élitist forms; for reasons perhaps no more compelling than habit, the iconography of Gilligan's Island apparently still commands less respect than that of the Renaissance, and rich industrialists, who used to endow chairs of literature or medieval history, are less eager to be memorialized by associations with advertising or "contemporary communications."

As for the social sciences, they have been part of the general rout of liberalism and social democracy. Thatcherism, neo-conservatism—call it what you will—was an intellectual victory as well as a political one and indeed that victory was partly driven by the failure of sociology and social engineering, especially its failure in the United States around race. It simply didn't work. And it's difficult to overemphasize how important this is.

113

The social sciences provided the university with its dominant ideology through the fifties, sixties and into the seventies, a liberalism that was, first and foremost, a crude anticommunism, but which also had some pretensions to social relevancy. The collapse of this, both practically and ideologically, left a huge vacuum within the university, largely filled today by "political correctness"—which can be seen, in many respects, as simply an attempt to achieve by fiat and coercion within the academy what the older "social engineering" couldn't outside. In any case, the social sciences are now a ruin; the last viable parts, reduced to a series of techniques, have been taken over by the "marketing" departments of business schools.

And finally, the university lost its value as a Cold War "asset." The military and intelligence communities, naturally enough, still have important academic connections, but the world has moved on. The relevant centres of political understanding are now on Wall Street, specialized "think tanks" and political/media consulting firms: which are, in effect, "spin-offs" from the academy.

Accordingly, the university, like Ms. Delorme, no longer attempts to justify itself in terms of its content—and it would fail if it tried: there's too little of it. So the discourse of promise has happily flourished here—and that's entirely appropriate, since the university is one of the most important promises of all. The university degree has now become a "right"; failure to receive it is a promise denied. Its form, defined by its egalitarianism, becomes its content, a tedious fundamentalism whose only "test" is adherence to its dogma: but that's all that can be required—where everyone must accomplish equally, no one accomplishes much of anything at all. Inevitably, the university's value declines, and for everyone; we care less and less about its demise, because there's less and less to care for. No doubt "bad" politicians, "right-wingers" like Mike Harris, will be blamed for "cuts"; but the real culprits are those who made those cuts so easy.

To conclude, one naturally wants to acknowledge the members of the university, both faculty and students, who still soldier on, at least seeking a genuine education, and perhaps finding bits of it. And it's possible to offer something of an honourable defence. The simple truth is that any university which placed merit and genuine achievement at the heart of its endeavour would inevitably reproduce the social stratification—the inequality—of the society around it; for the correlation between stratification and achievement is that ironclad. The democratic university, with broad accessibility, may well require low standards and minimal content. In any case, that's what we have today. But since it's not worth very much (and that worth is declining), we simply don't value it and are prepared to quietly watch its decline. Ironically, that decline will probably lead back toward an older élitism, a sharp stratification of schools something along American lines. Meanwhile, the current situation is an unmitigated disaster. Young people are being bankrupted to pay for this inferior, degraded institution. And even if we pretend to ignore it, I suspect we actually know what's going on. The loss of the university—one of the great promises we claimed to believe in, one of the true bedrocks of our faith, part of "the big promise"—is one we all feel. And it is part of the reason for our present malaise.

III

The fate of the vets and the fate of Canadian students—the past and present of the country—both mark and illustrate the collapse of the "big promise," and this very much defines our present situation. Like betrayed children, we are angry and bewildered. Our confidence has been critically shaken; we don't know where to turn. We can no longer *believe*. With our faith shattered, our voices are now hard with disillusionment.

But it's important to understand the differences between the two situations, and to see how they mirror two different aspects of *promise*. The vets came to define a kind of ideal citizen, and it was easy enough to then generalize from that ideal *to ourselves*— to extend to everyone, ordinary citizens, the same sense of responsibility felt toward the society's most exemplary members. But this depended, precisely, upon the idea and the practical reality of a common citizenship; and indeed the core of the welfare state is found around that commonality and citizenship, around services that *all* citizens require, such as education and medical care. But the discourse of promise has successfully displaced those older ideas, and accordingly has redefined the vets. They are now just one group among many, their "interests" defined by their "victimization" as most of the others are. It's important to remember that they haven't simply been displaced from their previous position as "ideal" citizens; the very notion of citizenship, which previously defined them, doesn't exist within *promise*. Of course, contemporary supporters of *promise* try to claim that the special rights/programs/benefits extended to various "special" groups are, so to speak, merely *additional to* the "rights" of their common citizenship; and in fact the position of Indians is often referred to as "citizenship plus." But practically and logically this new discourse contradicts the old.

For vets, the particular consequences of this have been seen: reduced to another "interest group" they are far more vulnerable than they were—the government can cut their benefits and get away with it. But, inevitably, that vulnerability extends to the general social developments of which they were a part. *The broad, universal programs of the welfare state such as medicare— "the social safety net"—are rendered extraordinarily vulnerable under the discourse of promise.* Those programs are universal; they are extended to all citizens, as an aspect of their citizenship. But *promise* always assumes some "special" need, interest, victimization: *it always assumes and seeks fragmentation.* The discourse of promise operates by the definition of special need so that special, compensating rights, benefits or privileges may be demanded. Given the triumph of this discourse, it therefore becomes reasonable to demand some proof of special need—a "means test," for example—as a precondition of pensions, medical care and so forth. Arguments against "universality" certainly predate the triumph of *promise*; but there is no doubt that *promise* enormously legitimizes them. Indeed, the discourse of promise (though often associated with "the left") has been far more important, ideologically, in undermining the Canadian welfare state than any of the more conventional arguments of "the right."

Students, it might be assumed, can be seen in the same way. And to a degree, obviously, they can. At least rhetorically, students have always been defined as something like an ideal, our "citizens of the future," and investment in their welfare has had the same sort of general, nonpartisan support that we associate with the vets. And surely the undermining, by *promise*, of the older notions of citizenship which define the fate of the vets has also been at work in regard to students. But in fact it's not the *fragmenting, incoherent* tendency of *promise* that's at work here; it's rooted, rather, very directly in the *childishness*, which, as we've seen, is a main source of emotional energy for this whole sort of discourse. Every aspect of *promise* is touched by this. It's built right into the language, in phrases like "election goodies"—treats promised to good little boys and girls. More profoundly, you can see it at work in the *victimization* that's so crucial to the working of *promise*: the image of the punished/abandoned/deserted child becomes the "ideal" victim, and indeed the "abused" child is a hallmark of the age. It was once said that Joe McCarthy could find a Red under every bed; today, a pedophile lurks there—and finds his equivalent in the "stalker," the "harasser,"* the brutal cop and all the other victimizing figures of the tabloid press, afternoon television and the advocacy groups petitioning for government funds.

But the particular aspect of this infantilization that touches students is more subtle than this. With children, it should be remembered, the act of making and receiving promises, of having promises fulfilled and betrayed, is at least as important as the content of the promises themselves. A promise is its own content—distinct from the particular occasion which gives rise to it.

---

* The evolution of feminism along this axis has been particularly fascinating. In the 1960s, feminism focused on the self-sufficiency of women and explicitly objected to the culture's tendency to infantilize them. Women wished to be seen as strong, adult, perhaps especially in regard to their sexual feelings. Today, by contrast, women insist on their relative weakness and vulnerability, their need for special treatment and protection; and sexuality is only discussed in terms of feminine victimization (at the hands of rapists, harassers and so on). Of course the previous tendency hasn't vanished—nothing in our political culture inhibits women from trying to have it both ways, indeed every way; but the shift in the balance has been dramatic and decisive.

For this reason, all promises tend to be equivalent—the medium is the message, form is a good deal of content. Promises all play the same role, bridging with trust the gulf between the adult parent and the child. They all tend to be absolute; they admit no qualification or exception: or, if they are broken, any explanation. This is how, at the level of the individual, "the big promise" is made.

In politics, this aspect of *promise* emerges in a number of ways, but in all cases it involves a devaluation of *content*. *Promise* always displaces the programmatic, the analytical, the systematic—part of its appeal, within contemporary politics, is that such questions no longer have to be addressed. And once a promise is made and "kept," there's relatively little *evaluation* of its effects. The announcement of a program, benefit, appointment or whatever—*we kept our promise*—is all that's politically required; whether anything is achieved by the promise is of minor consequence. Typically, political promises are evaluated only in terms of their narrow credibility—i.e., will they be carried out or not. The question of whether they might actually accomplish some legitimate social goal is almost completely passed over. Arguments about the GST, for example, and the failure of the Liberal Party to abolish it, rarely deal with the question of whether or not it's a good tax. Smart politicians now understand this. With the triumph of *promise*, individual promises increasingly have a merely formal role, affirming the system of which they are a part: for the population, sustaining their belief in "the big promise"; for the politician, defining him as trustworthy. And since the content of promises is of declining importance, and minimal promises are inherently more credible—more likely to be seen as capable of fulfilment—the *less* you promise, the better off you are. President Clinton, for example, made a number of small, essentially insignificant promises during his 1996 presidential campaign; they didn't amount to a program, but they cast him in the role of a believable, trustworthy politician and father (virtually all of his promises were justified in terms of children). Bob Dole, on the other hand, proposed a large tax cut that was part of a general economic program; but it gained him nothing.

The university today is part of this same syndrome. In a formal sense, the promise has been kept—it's there, the buildings are visible on the skyline; hundreds of thousands attend it each day. And arguments about it, as Ms. Delorme so clearly shows, focus solely on the question of whether even more should go, and on what terms. The fact that it's increasingly devoid of content is almost totally overlooked. But of course it can't be entirely overlooked. And so, as the value of what it offers diminishes year by year, society and governments value it less, fund it less . . . and no one cares. The university is taken less and less seriously; is seen less and less as a legitimate and important social institution. Its justification becomes increasingly nebulous. No one is quite certain why it exists or what purpose, in its contemporary form, it serves. It's a promise that hasn't been broken so much as forgotten. The political debates that circulate around it are largely about administrative questions, funding, academic privileges and such government measures as the "zero tolerance" policy of the NDP in Ontario (a quasi-legislated policy of "political correctness"). *Content*, substance, is always ignored. But that is part of *promise*. And the promise was never about knowledge, or understanding, or education—it was always about *going to university* and the advantages that would bestow. That promise, *as a promise*, has actually been kept; and to children, that's basically what counts. They never consider that in the world of *promises*, promises are increasingly meaningless.

But the particular fates of the vets and students under *promise* mustn't obscure their general importance. In them, we can see the erosion of "the big promise," which has been the foundation of our personal and social confidence. We can ignore what has happened in these particular cases, or pretend to, but we're all too aware that something fundamental is being lost, in society and ourselves. If this can happen, we know, everything is *not* all right. And so our anxiety, disillusionment and anger intensifies, souring everything.

The collapse of the "big promise" now conditions our politics in every way, and is the cause beneath all the other causes for our present distress. It's revealed, above all, in the tone and tenor of our political life, what Laurier La Pierre would call the state of our soul—which is now full of desperation. It's revealed in an almost universal distrust, suspicion and sense of grievance—we've been cheated. Most extraordinarily of all, it's revealed in a remarkable political nostalgia. We've lost the "big promise," but we still yearn for it, and so part of the appeal of a politician like Chrétien—as I'll show in a moment—is purely anachronistic. He harks back to a time when French Canadians were "pea-soupers" and "good government" meant a quiet political supervision of the civil service in Ottawa. With Preston Manning, this nostalgia achieves a kind of apotheosis. In a country of great cities—more urbanized, indeed, than the United States—he offers us the values of a rural, small-town world. To comprehend a modernity of extraordinary complexity, he confidently sets out the solutions of a radio preacher. He is the first English-Canadian politician in a generation to offer himself for high office while being absolutely, even aggressively, incompetent in French. Most revealing of all, he is the first populist to come out of the West since Diefenbaker, and one of his great causes is the restoration of capital punishment, which the old Chief so passionately opposed. And there's the clue. Diefenbaker was first elected in 1957. Manning's ideal world is the time before that, the glorious years of the fifties—when, in every highway and biway of the Dominion, "the big promise" seemed so clearly fulfilled. For so many today, that long-lost time—corresponding to the childhoods of so many baby-boomers—is the Golden Age, whose promise, a mirage, perpetually shimmers above a Lost Horizon.

Chapter Five

—◄o►—

Breaking Promises

*T*he failure of "the big promise" is the major feature of today's political landscape; it's the anxiety behind all the other anxieties, the particular issues that turn up on polls—jobs, medicare, crime and so on. As an Environics pollster put it, we have said "goodbye to the age of presumption and prosperity."[1] It's the reason for our frustration and malaise. And it's the reason behind the lack of trust generally felt for politicians. In truth, politicians today are neither more nor less trustworthy than their equivalents a generation ago; but since a promise has been broken, and it's always someone in particular who breaks a promise, they're *it*.

But it's also the reason for another defining feature of the present political moment, the tremendous anger people feel when politicians don't keep a *particular* promise. The general failure, that is, makes our anger at any particular breach of a promise all the more fierce. A case in point—one has to come back to it— is the GST. Even more particularly, the special case of Sheila Copps.

Tracking the history of Sheila and the GST not only allows us to define some of the general characteristics of *promise*, but shows us how it works in contemporary political practice.

The facts are simple enough. The GST, from the moment it was introduced, was unpopular—most new taxes are. The

Liberals, then in opposition, capitalized on this unpopularity by attacking the tax and promising to replace it. On April 4, 1990, Paul Martin put it plainly enough: "I would abolish the GST. The Manufacturers' Sales Tax is a bad tax, but there's no excuse to repeal one bad tax by bringing in another one." In the fall of that year, Jean Chrétien was equally explicit: "I am opposed to the GST, I have always been opposed to it and I will be opposed to it always."

True enough, in their official Red Book of election promises, the Liberals did introduce some fine print, a lawyerly gobbledy-gook of qualification: "A Liberal government will replace the GST with a system that generates equivalent revenues, is fairer to consumers and to small business, and promotes federal-provincial fiscal cooperation and harmonization." (Given this extraordinary range of virtues, it could have been dubbed the Miracle Tax.)

But this sort of qualification is always meaningless. Or, to put it another way, if the Liberals had expressed their intentions regarding the GST with this sort of language, they wouldn't have won a single vote. So, on a number of occasions, Jean Chrétien said that he would "kill" or "scrap" the tax, and when asked directly on a radio call-in show what he would do about the tax, said simply, "Yes, I would abolish it." And on the second of May, 1994—after the election, that is—he reiterated this: "We hate it, and we will kill it."

This was the sort of language senior Liberals used throughout the election—among lesser lights, it was even fiercer. I couldn't prove it, but I'd bet that every single Liberal candidate promised to abolish the tax; and two Liberal candidates were particularly clear about this: Sheila Copps and John Nunziata. Their names, of course, had long been linked, for they were members of the Liberal "Rat Pack" which had led the Liberals while in opposition.* Mr. Nunziata ran, and won, in York South–Weston on an unequivocal commitment to get rid of the tax, and on October 18, 1993, Sheila Copps said, "If the GST is not abolished under a Liberal government, I will resign."

But of course the tax wasn't abolished. And from the moment the Liberals took power, they were backtracking on their GST commitment. The exception—the crucial exception—was Mr. Nunziata. He continued to press for the abolition of the tax, and even worse, from the government's point of view, insisted on an unqualified, unambiguous interpretation of the government's policy. Having proved to be such a thorn in Mr. Mulroney's side, he was now an equally prickly proposition for Mr. Chrétien; it was certainly very difficult for the government to claim that they hadn't promised to abolish the tax when such a senior MP was insisting that they had. Ms. Copps, for her part, prevaricated. She squirmed, but of course Liberals are good at squirming. Moreover, she had been rewarded (unlike Mr. Nunziata) with a position in the government, no less a one than deputy prime minister, and was clearly not prepared to sacrifice it for a principle.

Matters came to a head in the spring of 1996.

When Paul Martin, the finance minister, brought down yet another budget which left the tax in place, Mr. Nunziata finally revolted: on April 12, he voted against the government on the budget motion. Mr. Chrétien reacted immediately. Without even giving Mr. Nunziata the opportunity to explain himself in

* The other members were Don Boudria and Brian Tobin.

person, he sent a fax to Mr. Nunziata's home, expelling him from the Liberal caucus. This swift response was undoubtedly an attempt to silence Mr. Nunziata for good and—in current jargon—"put the issue behind" the government. To the same end, Paul Martin attempted to blur and soften the government's position by finally admitting that "We made a mistake," though even this admission was instantly qualified: "It was a mistake in thinking we could bring in a completely different tax without undue economic distortion and within a reasonable period." And Mr. Chrétien, on April 24, demonstrated that his talents as a hair-splitting lawyer were still intact: "We are fulfilling the promise that we made as set out in the Red Book," he insisted. Having rid themselves of Mr. Nunziata, and having offered this parsimonious admission of failure, the only problem was Ms. Copps. Taking a cue from her political betters, she continued to fudge, and on April 25 offered this explanation of her position: "The fact is that when you're on the campaign trail, you get excited and sometimes you shoot from the lip. Did I make a mistake in making that statement? Yes. In the Catholic vernacular, it was venial not mortal. I think I should go to purgatory and not hell."

Although it must have been put together on the fly, this strategy would have seemed sensible enough. Mr. Nunziata's honesty had been redefined as rebelliousness and eccentricity; the government's position was still presented as being consistent with its original promise, only qualified by administrative realities ("within a reasonable time period") and the laudable desire to avoid "economic distortion"; and Ms. Copps's difficulties were to be understood only in terms of her tendency, undeniably the hallmark of her career, to overexcitement. All this should have worked for the Liberals. But it didn't. Within a week, the pressure on the government and Ms. Copps had become overwhelming, and she was compelled to resign. It was a resignation without honour or dignity. "Having failed to do the honourable thing," *The Globe and Mail* commented, "she has done the necessary one." And the whole episode, it went on, had "opened a gaping tear in the credibility of the government"; the only way to mend it was for Mr. Chrétien to come clean. "Voters may forgive failures," the *Globe* concluded, "they won't forgive lies."

This brought Act One of the shabby drama to a close. Taking a brief intermission, we can note a few points. The first is the extraordinary excitement around this utterly banal production. The plot couldn't have been more predictable, the cast more totally second-rate, the dialogue more pedestrian. I'm repeating myself, but it's an essential point: Liberal Party hacks were behaving like Liberal Party hacks—big deal. *Of course* the Liberal Party breaks its election promises, *of course* politicians lie: it's one of their principal professional skills. True, Mr. Nunziata's honesty was sufficiently quixotic to pique interest and Ms. Copps had something of a reputation as a "straight shooter"— so her discomfiture provided the media with opportunities for a little extra fun. And coming after the Mulroney years, the public was presumably less patient than usual. Nonetheless, the very fact that such a grand to-do was made of all this indicates that something out of the ordinary was going on. Everyone, including the public, was taken by surprise.

Underlining this was the reaction of the prime minister. No one will overestimate Mr. Chrétien; he is clearly the weakest Canadian prime minister elected since the Second World War. But no one can deny that he's an experienced and able politician. How could he have so misjudged the situation?

The answer lies in the sobriquet so often applied to him—he is Yesterday's Man. He's a politician who learned his trade in a different era; his hero, God help us, is Mitchell Sharp. When Mr. Chrétien first came to Ottawa, Mr. Sharp took him under his wing—wings that had learned to fly in the era of Mackenzie King and C.D. Howe. Sharp went back to 1942, when he joined the Department of Finance, and he was later deputy minister of the Department of Trade and Commerce, when Howe was the minister. After a stint in the private sector, he entered parliament in 1963—as did Chrétien. The two men became very close, and in the 1968 Liberal leadership campaign, Chrétien supported Sharp against Trudeau. Chrétien, in fact, has often described himself as "a Mitchell Sharp Liberal" and when he became prime minister, he asked Sharp to be a dollar-a-year adviser, and gave him an office in the PMO. Whether, in that capacity, Sharp gave his protégé advice about the GST crisis isn't known, but the strategy the prime minister adopted was probably one Sharp would have recognized and understood; it certainly harked back to his time. And in that earlier era, the strategy would likely have worked. But the discourse of promise has different rules; promises are no longer "cream puffs." Election promises mean something quite different today than they once did.

Part of that difference can be seen by taking a look at Act Two of our play, in which Ms. Copps ran in a by-election and won. And went right back into the cabinet. It was as if nothing had happened. As Preston Manning put it, "After all the fuss about the resignation, the GST is still there, and Sheila's back."[2]

But substantively nothing *had* happened. Because the substance, throughout, had been wholly emotional, beginning with the GST promise itself. It was never an "issue." There was never anything to "argue" about. It wasn't a "question" with "sides." It wasn't even a symbol, it was . . . well, a promise. It was a contract, with childish hopes on one side, and a childish omnipotence on the other. By resigning—*with all the fuss*—Ms. Copps stooped back down to this level. She was like an American evangelist caught with her hand in the till who tearfully apologizes and begs forgiveness on television; or, indeed, like a parent apologizing to her kids. *I know I promised to take you to the CNE today and I really meant to, but* . . . And of course her constituents were happy to forgive her. By means of this astonishing fandango, Ms. Copps completely defused the issue, *as it applied to herself.* In other words, she accepted and acted in accord with the discourse of promise, transforming a political issue into one that was purely personal and emotional.

Mr. Chrétien, however, still didn't get it. He clearly hoped and expected that *l'affaire Copps* would put an end to *l'affaire GST.* But it didn't. Of course, from Mr. Chrétien's point of view, the whole business must have seemed utterly irrational. So far as he was concerned, he had made an election promise, in the old-fashioned sense. It had been made to exploit a weakness of his opponent; it had been hedged adequately with fine print—clearly indicating that it would never actually be "kept"; and his government, in office, had "covered itself" by its various attempts to "harmonize" the tax with the provincial sales taxes. Could Mitchell Sharp have done better? Could Mackenzie King? No. And so it was an issue that should have faded away, especially given the extraordinary price paid by Ms. Copps. Accordingly he simply carried on as before, although even he must have seen the absurdity of this. He was claiming that the Red Book promise had been fulfilled despite the fact that his deputy prime minister had resigned her seat in recognition that it had not.

This set the stage for the last act, the famous "town hall" meeting on the CBC. Johanne Savoie, a waitress from Montreal, confronted the prime minister with his GST promise. She had, she said, voted for the Liberals because of their promise to abolish the GST—and, she made very clear, "I didn't hear tinker. I heard scrap." The prime minister's reply was, from his point of view, quite reasonable. He said she should have read the Red Book, with its fine print. He had carried out that "promise" to the letter.

The roof fell in on him.

From coast to coast, editorial page to phone-in show, the prime minister was attacked and condemned: Rafe Mair went after him, Gilbert Lavoie went after him, everyone went after him. Within days, he was swept into a major political crisis. And he compounded it by weaseling; instead of straightforwardly apologizing, he admitted making "an honest mistake," said he was sorry for any "confusion"—but never actually came clean.

His most revelatory gaffe concerned the town hall meeting itself. He accused the CBC of rigging it, of setting up an ambush. It wasn't "a real town hall," he claimed, "they had the questions prepared before."

The CBC's reply shows that Mr. Chrétien had, here as elsewhere—everywhere—actually been ambushed by the discourse of promise. This is sufficiently important to note in some detail, and here's part of the *Globe*'s report on that aspect of the controversy:

In the wake of the town hall meeting on Tuesday, the Liberal spin machine abruptly shifted into overdrive to portray the

CBC gathering as an orchestrated ambush on Mr. Chrétien. Strategists and even cabinet members have been suggesting in off-the-record interviews that the CBC stacked the audience with Canadians who have an axe to grind.

That's nonsense, says Tony Burman, executive producer of *The National* and the CBC official who oversees the town hall events. He says the questions reflected concerns of many Canadians, even those who support the government.

. . . The bulk of the audience is selected at random by an outside agency. In effect, these people are brought in simply to fill chairs. They are not allowed to ask questions, although they can have an effect on the tone of the broadcasts through the extent to which they laugh or applaud or even roll their eyes.

The process for selecting those who address queries to Mr. Chrétien is more subjective, and herein reside the ingredients of the Liberals' beef—although, Mr. Burman points out, they have never complained before.

Participants who ask a question are not selected randomly. Instead, a *National* staff member comes up with a list of candidates. This is accomplished by getting in touch with people across the country—reporters, business leaders and social activists among many others—and asking if they know anyone who would be a good participant.

What kind of person is the CBC looking for? Someone articulate, not afraid to go on television, and not directly involved with a political party . . . There is also the matter of gender, racial and regional representation. The CBC tries to include at least one participant from each province. And there is no guarantee that the person will be a so-called average Canadian. For instance, Juanita Mackeigen of Louisburg, N.S., who asked about job creation, has done a lot of public speaking and dealt with the news media as a representative of a fishery workers' union on Cape Breton.[3]

The report goes on, but I'll leave it there with the comment that, in terms of the quarrel with Mr. Chrétien, the CBC is entirely exonerated. From our point of view, however, we can see that this is all a perfect reflection of politics in the age of *promise.* The public is there anonymously to fill chairs; not allowed to speak for themselves, they are at least permitted to roll their eyes—this is a democracy, after all. Typically, the people who speak *for* them are members of advocacy groups—interestingly, people whose "politics" are not sufficiently organized to have caused them to join a political party; and of course they are not joined by a common citizenship, but rather divided by ethnicity, race, sex and so forth. The questions such people could ask, taken as a whole, can only reflect incoherence, are bound to be essentially emotional, and scarcely offer the opportunity for the rational discussion of politics at all. Indeed, such a program is a kind of equivalent to television wrestling, a false contest featuring mock participants. Mr. Chrétien and the Liberals certainly knew this—but Mr. Chrétien, apparently, didn't quite understand the consequences. And this was reflected in the particular exchange which gave Mr. Chrétien such difficulty. When Johanne Savoie asked about the GST, she was in fact expressing her *feelings*; Mr. Chrétien's reply treated this as a statement about her thinking, and was phrased accordingly. This made him seem *unfeeling.* And in fact he was.

How should Mr. Chrétien have replied? How should he have handled this whole affair?

An "honest" response was scarcely possible, given the dishonesty of the entire enterprise. The Red Book states, clearly enough, that the Liberals intended to replace the tax with "a system that generates equivalent revenues" and would be harmonized with the provinces. "System," in this statement, can only be a euphemism for "tax," unless the Liberals were contemplating the invention of some entirely novel way of taking money from us. But this equivalent tax couldn't have been, say, an increase in the income tax, because that wouldn't have required "harmonization" with the provinces: only a "sales" tax of some sort would have brought the provinces into it. Read carefully, the Red Book promise is pure nonsense; it actually says that the Liberals intended to replace the GST with the GST—there's no other reasonable construction you can put on it, and of course that's what Mr. Chrétien has actually done. If he'd in fact *argued* against the tax—on the grounds, perhaps, that consumption taxes are somewhat more regressive than income taxes—he might have had an easier time. He could have claimed that, upon reflection, he had decided that his argument was wrong. He could then have taken the high road, nicely laid out for him by an editorial in *The Financial Post*, which offered a fine quotation from Abraham Lincoln: *As bad promises are better broken than kept, I shall treat this as a bad promise, and break it, whenever I shall be convinced that keeping it is adverse to the public interest.*[4] But following this option would, in effect, have said: Brian Mulroney was right—and that would have been too much for Mr. Chrétien to swallow.

Tactically, the solution was actually easy enough. Mr. Chrétien simply needed to humble himself, rather as Ms. Copps had done. Since the whole business was an essentially emotional and symbolic transaction, he should have treated it that way. He should have confessed, abased himself, and promised to do better in the future. Even good little guys from Shawinigan can go wrong, he could have said, but, hopefully, if they work real hard they can regain people's faith. Done with skill—as Bill Clinton would have done—Mr. Chrétien's elevation in the polls would have been a certainty.

Why didn't he take this course? Again, I think we have to remember that Mr. Chrétien's political definition actually runs back a long way. He goes back to a time when prime ministers were supposed to be dignified, wear homburg hats and dark suits—his "ordinary joe" image actually plays off this, and so confirms it. In that era, prime ministers could never admit error or failure; above all, they had to be strong, *decisive.*

In many ways, this sorry episode allows us to trace the whole story of *promise.* For most of this country's history, political promises were electoral promises, and were merely an element in patronage politics. They were about docks and breakwaters, contracts for roads and bridges. Such promises weren't made, in the modern sense, to "create jobs"; rather, they worked to cement local political alliances, to reward and induce support in local political machines. They were little better than dressed-up bribes—and sometimes were entirely naked. But as the electoral system changed—as it became necessary for politicians to speak directly to voters, especially on television—promises became a key aspect in a different kind of discourse, one that trapped the leader and the electorate in a web of faith and emotion. Mr. Chrétien's career, a little anomalously, bridged the latter part of the older history and the new. His personal style, by virtue of its roughness and Mr. Chrétien's "common touch," fitted well with the new discourse, at least to a point; but his actual conduct of government, with his reliance on the public service, hands-on ministers and limitless pragmatism, harked back to the previous age. It was this contradiction that tripped him up. One can even speculate that another moment in his autobiography proved a problem. Mr. Chrétien entered parliament in the 1960s, with Mr. Pearson. His political instincts were formed and nurtured in a time when the "big promise" seemed capable of limitless fulfilment. Perhaps, as a figure from that age, he initially had a certain appeal—by bringing him back, it might have seemed possible to recapture that optimistic time. But of course history doesn't work like that. By 1996, the "big promise" had been broken, and people lived with a profound loss of faith. This meant that the breach of any particular promise would be given a special importance, and that's what happened around the GST. Promise bit one of the hands that had fed it. As Mr. Chrétien finally fled the country and headed for Asia, he must have wondered whether the bite was rabid.

Chapter Six

—◄o►—

The Negative Promise

*A*s a writer, I am naturally well disposed toward book-sellers, those soldiers at the pointy end of the book wars; and one of my favourites is a man named Paul King, who runs Food For Thought Books, in Ottawa. Mostly, being literary men, we talk about women and politics, but we also play golf, and one day, in the spring of 1995, we were hitting balls into the woods around a course on the Quebec side of the river while discussing the Ontario provincial election, then just commenced. This was appropriate. Bill Harris, the man the Tories were running, was a golfer.

"No," said Paul, "his name is Mike."

"Mike, Bob, Bill, Dave . . . surely they're all the same. Anyway, he's hopeless." In fact, at this early point in the campaign, the clear winner was going to be a female clone named "Lyn"— *The Toronto Star* and the news editors at the CBC had decided for us. Rae, the NDP premier, was low in the polls, and the Liberals, with their politically correct lady at the helm, were to step back into power. "Every time I've seen him," I went on, still thinking of Harris, "he babbles away about the Employer's Health Tax—no one knows what he's talking about."

"Don't you?"

"Yes, but I'm incorporated. I *pay* it."

"Yeah, but so is everybody else. Rae thinks 'corporation' means Imperial Oil, so he never understood how much people hated that tax—especially when they have to go to NDP parties and hear people defending 'free' health care. You watch, Harris is going to win." And then Paul—who can find balls in even the deepest brush—headed off to retrieve.

He was right, of course, and was the first person I knew who sensed the current that was carrying Harris to power. Three issues did it for him; *cut* taxes, *cut* welfare, *cut* government. In others words, he exemplified the power of *promise*—in its *negative* aspect. In today's politics, nothing could be more fashionable.

Harris, as everyone knows, wasn't the first: he was preceded by Ralph Klein, the rumpled premier of Alberta and—in different ways and to different degrees—by Gary Filmon in Manitoba and Roy Romanow in Saskatchewan. All of these premiers cut budgets and services to bring deficits under control; Romanow, for example, has eliminated more than a hundred hospitals in Saskatchewan. But Ralph Klein was especially important—not simply because he was first, but because the crucial element in his case was important in all the others.

That element, of course, is economic anxiety. It's possible to see the victory of Mike Harris in ideological terms, the triumph of the right, but that's not true with Ralph Klein. He is a Conservative premier succeeding a Conservative premier—Don Getty. Getty probably wasn't far enough to the right for many members of his party, but that wasn't the reason for his failure. Getty was a weak, ineffective politician; he had few ideas of his own, and almost no capacity to manage government. His downfall was the result of his obvious personal failings, and two important economic developments. The first was the decline of the oil economy, so important in Alberta, and the second was the collapse of the Principal Group, a provincially regulated financial institution.

For Albertans, these developments gave a hard-edged definition to the failure of the "big promise." The strength of the oil economy, whose revenues created Peter Lougheed's "Heritage Fund," was the concrete basis for Alberta's self-confidence—and a sprawling, generous provincial government. (When Klein came to power, Alberta had more provincial and municipal employees per capita than any other province in the country.) The province was able to fund a terrific hospital system and actually provide *grants**to university students, while maintaining a very low tax structure, with no sales tax at all. Although most Canadians traditionally view Alberta as being "antigovernment," this isn't as simple as it sounds. Under Peter Lougheed, "the government was seen as the tool to lead and guide economic growth. A generation of bright young Albertans headed from universities into public service. The Lougheed Conservatives had spread provincial offices and employees around rural Alberta to pump up local economies."[1] The consequences, naturally, involved rapid spending growth, sometimes as high as 17 per cent a year. "The Conservative governments of the Lougheed era had built their style and their philosophy around more spending and a bigger government presence"[2]—which is to say, they were trying to deliver on "the big promise" in a fairly traditional way.

---

* Since Klein became premier, the grants have ended. He has cut spending on education by over 20 per cent.

But of course this was all dependent on high oil and gas royalties. When these weakened—and after Getty had squandered huge sums on various unwise investments, especially NovAtel ($600 million)—the government was driven into a continuously worsening deficit position.

This created real concern at the public level. But then this was compounded by the collapse of the Principal Group, which cost thousands of ordinary Albertans their pension investments—and made them completely lose confidence in the Conservatives, who'd been ruling for more than twenty years. Indeed, this was the reason Getty brought Klein into provincial politics—a search for fresh blood—though it didn't do the premier much good; in the election of 1989, he actually lost his own seat in Edmonton and had to come back into the legislature via a by-election. By the time he finally resigned, and Klein took the leadership, the Conservatives were more than 15 per cent behind the provincial Liberals in the polls.

This is the background of "the Klein revolution" and it's a background of panic. He responded that way—in a kind of frenzy. Within three months of taking office, he had purged the cabinet, wiped out whole departments of government, cut ministerial salaries and was firing civil servants left, right and centre. The revolution had begun. But it wasn't a revolution—"it was a restoration every bit as dramatic and far-reaching for Alberta as was the restoration of King Charles II for the English . . . Klein had intuitively and accurately connected to the deepest roots of Alberta politics and one of its oldest and strongest tribal memories: the memory of government indebtedness and insolvency."[3]

To understand the panic which Klein took advantage of, you have to understand that tribal memory. It goes back to the

Depression, the Dust Bowl years that devastated the West, including Alberta—a devastation that destroyed farms and lives, but also government finances: in fact the provincial government was literally bankrupt during the 1930s and '40s. When Social Credit came to power in 1935, Alberta was $385 million in debt, couldn't pay the interest it owed on that debt, and was surviving on loans advanced by the feds. But when Mackenzie King created the Dominion Provincial Loan Council, Alberta refused to join, and in 1936 began defaulting on its bonds; indeed, by the end of that year, the province's securities were barred from trading on the London Stock Exchange. It wasn't until after the war, when the appeal of social credit doctrine had diminished in the bosom of Ernest Manning and his faithful followers, that the province was able to re-establish itself as a legitimate borrower. From that point on, fiscal conservatism became the norm. "Never again, determined Manning, would the province live beyond its means. For twenty-five years, he balanced the books, improved and expanded education and health care facilities, and built a frugal system of social welfare that provided basic care for the needy." As one commentator put it, "The parallels between Manning's situation and Ralph Klein's in December of 1992 are uncanny."[4]

The Negative Promise

Klein skilfully capitalized on this. In a sense, he didn't have to convince anyone about his policies or programs; people *knew,* viscerally. Klein's "revolution" had nothing to do with new ideas, but old ones; he wasn't breaking new ground, merely returning to familiar paths. Although frequently justified with the new buzz words—"globalism," "interdependence" and so forth—Ralph Klein had effectively turned back the clock. His negative promises only recalled Manning's true faith. Thus, Klein's policies could never be the "model" for anyone else's, or only to a limited degree; they were ultimately dependent on the very particular history of his province. But they did contain one element that other "negative promisers" have needed: *a sense of financial and economic panic, a sense at both the public and personal level that things were out of control.*

To understand the situation that faced Mike Harris in Ontario, it's useful to bear in mind the Alberta experience—but there were some different factors as well. Tribal memory, for one thing. Ontario has always been the most complacent of the Canadian provinces, confident, drearily smug. Its politics has never been happy with ideology; like a good, law-abiding driver, it has always stayed to the right of the centre line—but has usually stayed on the road. With Mike Harris, however, that seems to have changed. His detractors certainly always describe him in ideological terms—"Gingrichian," for example. He is clearly far more ideological than most of his Conservative predecessors, men like Bill Davis. Moreover, his government has followed a government of the left. And indeed the shift from a social democrat like Bob Rae to a conservative like Mike Harris provides, for analytical purposes, the great virtue of contrast.

This is especially so because Rae's government so perfectly exemplified *promise.* Up to a point, even he sees this. In the conclusion to his memoirs, he writes: "In opposition, it was easy for the party to become allied with groups preoccupied by one issue or another. The television culture of our times has also fostered time and attention for articulate speakers on behalf of a single cause. Yet governing is necessarily about reconciling competing interests . . . A political party has to be more than a rag bag of complaints and grievances if it wants to govern."[5]

Coming at the end of his book, this presumably is hindsight, for even at the very beginning of his government it's easy to see that the "television culture"—which is really the discourse of promise—was his culture, too. At his swearing in, he said, "The new government that is taking office today is made up of *women and men* from across the province, from all walks of life." In the discourse of promise—the television culture—"women and men" is not only more politically correct than "men and women," it's more correct than *Canadians*, which would have fitted his meaning here without any reference to "gender," at all. Rae was perfectly comfortable with this: his government made sexual harassment, employment "equity" (quotas) and other issues from "the rag bag" of the advocacy groups the major concerns of his politics. Often enough, he claims that he tried to govern for everyone in the province, but in fact his government was completely dominated by groups who'd defined themselves in terms of *promise*.[†] Ultimately, there was a revelatory irony here. The hallmark of his regime, at least in its latter years, was something called *The Social Contract*. No doubt Rae was sufficiently well educated to know that this phrase, and concept, referred to the relations between the state and *the whole of society*. In Rae's Ontario, however, the public-service unions were the only group to which it applied—and that defined the *only society* he was concerned with. Still, appropriately—and this is

The Negative Promise

---

† At the same time, it's important to remember that Rae's government wasn't dominated by "special interests" in any excessive way—most previous Ontario governments had been dominated by business, an "interest" no less special than any other. But the method of definition was very different.

the irony—he taxed them accordingly; a special-interest group was made to suffer in the name of society as a whole.‡

Rae, it should be noted, embraced the discourse of promise because he believes in it. The fragmentation of society which it reflects and represents he considers inevitable, conceivably desirable. "We live now not so much in a national economy as in a series of regional economies increasingly linked to global interdependence . . . The phrase 'global village' was invented in the 1960s by Marshall McLuhan. Thirty years later it is closer to a reality." And, in a kind of inverted way, he even sees this as contributing to his demise. Writing of his defeat, he says, "Harris succeeded in a time-tested, right-wing populist way, by touching the buttons of resentment about taxes, welfare, race, and gender . . . If he successfully maintains the resentments that divide people, he may also continue to govern."

Of course, this isn't why Harris won, nor is it generally why Canadian populists win. Canadian populists (even right-wing populists) don't play on the divisions of race and "gender," or any other divisions, with the exception (in extreme cases) of language and religion; they appeal, rather, to people's desire for unity, their desire to belong to a community—to identify with *my fellow Canadians*, as one Conservative populist put it. It was, in fact, Mr. Rae's government that had made race, "gender" and so forth divisive; his government positively revelled in such division; moreover, this had been done in the name of abstruse, implausible, Orwellian theories—"affirmative action," or "positive discrimination," for example—invariably advanced by

---

‡ I say "tax": in effect, that's what "Rae days" amounted to, although Mr. Rae justifies them on grounds of "work sharing."

"experts" of one sort or another. Over and against this, Mr. Harris simply appealed to basic notions of fairness, antidiscrimination and equality before the law—notions dunned into the population over centuries, and indeed constituting the basis of the social contract in its Lockean, pre–Bob Rae sense. Mr. Harris, apparently a fan of the Hardy Boys, doesn't pretend to be an intellectual and didn't justify these ideas in any elaborate way, but rather appealed to people's *common sense*. Indeed, the particular quality of Mr. Rae's government was to make common sense seem revolutionary, thereby providing a tissue of plausibility to Mr. Harris's favourite slogan, *the common sense revolution*. Finally, Mr. Harris had a great piece of luck. The mass media overwhelmingly plumped for Lyn McLeod. The fix was in. The fix was so obviously in that it stank up the joint. Rae's campaign was doomed. Lyn McLeod was too obviously the choice of the Powers That Be. The people, exercising their democratic rights, rolled their eyes, and Mr. Harris romped home.

But this account of Mr. Harris's triumph—and this sort of triumph in general—must be handled carefully.

At first glance, it would seem to be a victory against *promise*. In general, Mr. Harris certainly presented himself as a representative of older, more traditional ideas of citizenship. And although liberals like Mr. Rae have abandoned them, large numbers of people still do believe in a meaningful distinction between the sexes, think discrimination of any kind abhorrent, and find simple arithmetic a useful adjunct to financial calculation. But this, effectively, is nostalgia. It is one more testimony to the effect the loss of "the big promise" has had, and is the real source of the resentment that Mr. Rae, in his account, correctly notes. Anger against taxes is largely an expression of anger (and anxiety) about falling incomes. Distrust of "employment equity" is a worry about departing from traditional values, but also a suspicion that peculiar political norms will somehow be used to deprive me of my job—in a time of rising unemployment. And anger at large increases to welfare recipients (especially among the working poor, who often found themselves earning less) expresses a fear about falling into that abyss yourself.

Mr. Harris was able to mobilize these resentments and connect them, superficially, to the loss of older values; but those older values were no longer able to support a *positive* program, or in any case they weren't asked to. For Mr. Harris's "promises" were entirely *negative*. In June of 1996, Mr. Harris issued "A First-Year Report Card on the Ontario Government" which lists his "Promises Kept," and most involved words like "cut," "reduce" or "repeal." Others were merely the staple bromides of provincial politics—"Boost the volunteer sector"—or, at best, concerned the maintenance of existing programs: "Protect and enhance health care" or "Increase funding for children in need."

So, at the highest level, Harris's politics was the shadow cast by the failure of "the big promise"—rather than rejecting *promise*, as he seemed to do, Harris (like Klein) actually exemplified it, only in a negative way. Moreover, at the tactical level, he exploited it with considerable skill. Promises, as we have seen, are normally allied with wishes and hopes and positive expectations; but they can be threats and forebodings, too—*promise me you won't do that ever again!* Harris's negative promises were like this, and capitalized on the prevailing negativity to seem more credible.

It is here that the role of economic anxiety comes into play.

Ontario's finances were in very poor shape, as a result of the slump of the early nineties and the Rae government's inept response to it. Faced with a declining economy and a worsening fiscal situation, Rae's first budget massively increased already large deficits in a ludicrous Keynesian exercise in "stimulation"—ludicrous, because there was nothing Ontario could do that would isolate it from a trade depression that had swept over the entire Western world. This quickly produced deficits so large that even Mr. Rae noticed. But instead of cutting government programs and firing civil servants—a straightforward, comprehensible response—he embarked on the drawn-out, tortuous exercise of "the social contract." The province, as a whole, found this confusing and unsettling; and when civil servants began striking and demonstrating, the situation began to look frightening, out of control. Mr. Rae had done precisely what he ought not to have done: turned a bad situation into a general crisis.

All this helped defeat the Rae government, but, even more importantly, became the background against which the Harris government acted. The population was now convinced that the province was on the edge of bankruptcy, or something very close to it, which certainly made *cuts* to spending seem more believable and sensible than promises of plump new programs. In office, Harris also understood the effect of breaking even the smallest promise—that is to say, he had learned (or understood instinctively) the lesson taught by Sheila Copps. Disappointed so often, the public was waiting for the opportunity to pounce on the slightest breach of faith. The test case for Mr. Harris concerned the installation, by the previous government, of "photo radar" on major highways, especially Highway 401 around Toronto. In opposition, Harris had attacked these as simply another tax on drivers, while the government, the police and various advocacy groups had defended them as a legitimate safety measure. Once elected, there was a good deal of pressure on Harris to keep the radars in place, and some evidence that he wavered—since, no doubt, the radars function *both* as a tax *and* a safety measure. But he had the good (political) sense to hold fast, and get rid of them, considerably enhancing his credibility.

Credibility—this has been the watchword for politicians like Mike Harris. *Doing What We Said We'd Do*: so reads a headline on the Harris "Report Card." Both Mr. Harris and Mr. Klein have been careful "to keep their promises" and make a point of underlining this at every opportunity. They have become, so they would have it, exponents of "tough love"—a favourite catchword, which of course comes from a pop-psychology technique for dealing with difficult children. Because their promises are negative, they are easy to fulfil, or at least capable of fulfilment—hence credible. This credibility is further reinforced by a rather rough-and-ready personal style, which can be seen in both Mr. Harris and Mr. Klein. The combination—negative promises, "bad news," delivered in this sincere way—is enormously effective; you can't quote TV news interviews, but take my word for it, I've seen people who've lost their jobs because of Mr. Harris actually say "well, at least he's keeping his promise."

But, it must be emphasized, all this is still within the discourse of promise—very much so. *Promise* always defines political leaders in terms of "character issues," such as credibility and trustworthiness. These become issues in themselves, so that the *substance* of promises are overlooked or downplayed, and all other political qualifications—skill, experience—are neglected entirely. Sincerity becomes everything. Of course, the whole process is self-reinforcing and self-validating . . . but it's the same old process.

More substantively, you can see this at the very heart of Mr. Harris's politics. He would, of course, refuse to concede that his promises are "negative" and would doubtless point out that his most important *cut* is a cut in taxes, and that this constitutes part of a positive program of economic development.

There are two interesting points here.

One should, of course, hope that Mr. Harris is right. Certainly the constant rise in taxes over recent years hasn't created prosperity—cutting taxes might well. But Mr. Harris's tax cuts—and Preston Manning's, and Jean Charest's—in fact constitute a means of rationalizing *cuts in government spending*. They are rewards for a massive reduction in the size and scope of government. Politicians like Mr. Harris pursue this, of course, as an end in itself, and argue for it. Government is too large. Government is ineffective. "Big government"—an integral part of "the big promise"—is a failure. A principal proof of this failure is the size of governments' annual deficits, and the overall size of the public debt. *Chronologically*, it is the deficit and the debt that came first—and the chronology I'm thinking of here is political as much as economic. Beginning with Michael Wilson and Brian Mulroney, politicians at all levels (and of all ideological persuasions) have gradually convinced Canadians that the fiscal situation of Canadian governments has become catastrophic. Remember the case of Ralph Klein—here is the major common denominator between his case and Ontario's. But here we also find a curious point. The people are now so convinced of this situation that they find promises of tax cuts unbelievable and, to a degree, irresponsible. There was enormous scepticism in Ontario about Mr. Harris's promised tax cut, and a widespread refusal to believe that he would actually implement it. And, when he did, he didn't get much credit for it. In the same way, the federal Conservatives' tax-cut proposal, prepared for the 1997 election, met almost total incredulity; and Mr. Manning's (although worked out in great detail) hasn't enjoyed a much happier fate. On the other hand, *cuts in government spending* have, increasingly, become a political issue. Beyond a certain point, Ralph Klein's cuts in Alberta provoked real opposition, sufficiently powerful that he began to revoke them. And Mr. Harris's government became so concerned about the public's anxiety around spending cuts (especially to health care) that he mounted a major advertising campaign to combat it. My point here is not to judge Mr. Harris—rather, to show that the discourse of promise in his politics remains very much intact. *Negative* promises are promises nonetheless. Mr. Harris is wearing a different-coloured uniform but he's still playing the game. Ultimately, he will be judged the way everyone else has been judged. The Canadian people still expect their politicians and governments to fulfil "the big promise," *to make everything all right.* After all the years of *promise,* they literally don't know what else to expect.

So negative promises are promises, too. The fact that they are more immediately credible doesn't relieve the promisor of a fundamental obligation, an obligation that extends beyond the particular content of what they are saying. By engaging in the discourse of promise, people like Mike Harris and Ralph Klein are nonetheless committing themselves to the "big promise"— even though the failure of that promise is partly what has created the circumstances for their own success. In some ways, their credibility, so carefully cultivated, makes their situation more difficult; it's been achieved by imposing sacrifice—if everything isn't all right in the end, they risk a wrath even greater than their more conventional predecessors have suffered. In their particular cases, perhaps, that won't happen; they'll simply pass from the stage. It's extremely difficult to move from a politics based around negative promises to something more positive. In truth, they don't really wish to. Politicians like Harris and Klein—and Preston Manning at the federal level—can't do anything else *but* cut. The underlying dynamic of their politics insists that taxes can never be too low, that spending is always too high. Klein, in particular, has explicitly rationalized his approach by an analysis of the global situation which sees Alberta, and Canada as a whole, competing economically in a progressively more integrated capitalist world. Of course, that analysis is correct. But their solution is to depress wages and taxes, thereby making their jurisdictions attractive to investment—and so creating "prosperity" of a sort. In effect, Canada becomes the Mexico of the north. The alternative strategy—to become some equivalent to Austria, say, or Switzerland—would require a rather different approach. It would certainly emphasize fiscal responsibility. But it would also try to find a relative competitive advantage in a more highly skilled and educated labour force equipped with superior capital. But—thinking of provincial politicians—this would imply massive additional spending on education and training. Naturally, both Klein and Harris pay lip service to the importance of education, as all politicians must do. But among Klein's first acts as premier was the celebration, as part of "the Alberta Advantage," of the lowest minimum wage in the country (save Newfoundland and Prince Edward Island) and his first cuts chopped kindergarten out of the school system and elimi-nated grants to university students. As for Harris, his education minister is a high-school dropout, one of whose first acts was the elimination of an entire grade from the school system (more efficient, of course).

But it's obviously unfair to look to Klein, Harris and Man-ning for a positive vision of government. Their careers have been based on the failure of precisely that vision, which has been part of the general failure of *promise*. They are one side of the coin; on the other are all those politicians whose promises have dashed hope, belief and faith. These days, as the coin flips over and over in the air, our frustration is so great that it hardly seems to make any difference which way it lands.

Chapter Seven

—◄o►—

Ending the Discourse?

*T*oday, Canadian politics is dominated by the discourse of promise—and by frustration and failure.

Two of our great political parties, the Conservatives and the New Democrats, tiptoe along the brink of extinction. For a whole parliament, the Opposition was led by a group whose sole goal is the destruction of the country and which, if M. Parizeau is to be believed, was an element in a conspiracy with a foreign power to destroy Canadian sovereignty. Politicians are universally abominated. Politics, as a way of defining ourselves and dealing with our problems, is barely a joke. Political debate? It doesn't exist. Obsessively, compulsively, we return to the same "issues" and get nowhere with them. But we have no right to be surprised at this. Officially, Canada speaks two languages, but in our politics there's only the language of *promise*, a language rooted in childhood and eschatology—so it's inevitable that our political processes tend toward the infantile and apocalyptic.

The frustration, of course, is generally felt. Everyone *says* they want to get out of it. Bob Rae, realizing too late what it has done to him, tries to protest against it—but the only words he can find belong to the same language that choked him in the first place. Politicians like Harris and Klein, with their *negative* promises, *pretend* to be different: but they're just the other side

of the same old coin. And most of our publicly elected "repre-
sentatives," regardless of what they say, carry on as before—

though presumably Sheila Copps will watch her mouth a little
more closely.

A mark of this frustration—and an indication of how very
dangerous it is—can be found in one of the more curious features of our contemporary situation. Two important political
formations, the Reform Party on the one hand and the Bloc
Québécois/Parti Québécois on the other, both have *referendums*
as major elements in their political programs. Referendums do
have a political history in Canada, but only a slight one—
they've never been a regular part of our political process, and
have no particular constitutional role; at best they've served as a
political convenience. So why have they taken on special importance now?

Of course, the Reform Party and the separatists have a great
deal in common. Both are hinterland parties led by hinterland
politicians. Both practise the discourse of promise in a particularly fantastical way—on the one hand, offering the promise of
a new country in a never-never-land future, on the other, a
"fresh start" in a golden, childish past, the world of the fifties
when the top-rated TV show was "The Wonderful World of Dis-
ney." And they have common roots of an even more particular,
concrete sort. The Reform Party, led by Preston Manning, is a
reinvention of his father's Social Credit—whose base in Quebec,
during the great days of Réal Caouette, is the separatist heartland today. Mr. Manning's Reform plays mightily on hating the
French—M. Bouchard's separatists on hating the English. In
many respects, then, this is the same political train, just moving
through the station in opposite directions.

Referendums also play a similar role for both the separatists and Reform. In both cases, they are seen as a way of bringing political discourse to an end, in effect a way of *breaking* with the frustrations the current discourse creates. In Mr. Manning's case, the connection to *promise* couldn't be clearer. Here's how he introduces "A Fresh Start on Accountability," the section of the Reform program that talks about referendums, recall and citizens' initiatives:

> These days, people put little faith in the promises of politicians. And for good reason. Every time an election campaign comes around, so do the politicians, making all kinds of promises that are almost sure to be broken when no longer convenient.
>
> Reform is offering something completely different. Our commitment to implement our platform is not based on promises, but on a real democratic guarantee. We will give you the right to fire any one of our MPs if they do not do what they say they are going to do. We believe it's the fresh approach to politics Canadians are looking for.

The program then defines what this "accountability" will consist of and how it will be achieved:

> A Reform Government will:
>
> Give you the tools to ensure that we keep our promises. We will bring in workable recall for federal politicians, to hold us accountable to our constituents for the commitments we make to Canadians.

Replace the current undemocratic, unrepresentative Senate with a Senate that is elected, equal and effective.

Give voters direct input into decision-making through referendums and citizens' initiatives on important issues.[1]*

A number of points should be made here.

First, note how carefully Mr. Manning tries to distance himself from *promise*. He directly says *our platform is not based on promises*, but of course it is, and in fact "accountability" means giving *you the tools to ensure that we keep our promises.* Indeed, rather than breaking with the discourse of promise, Mr. Manning's suggestions mire us more deeply in it. *Keeping promises* now becomes the most important, even the sole, definition of the politician's role. The possibility of political leadership is virtually extinguished, and there's no room for a man like Abraham Lincoln: *I shall treat this as a bad promise, and break it, whenever I shall be convinced that keeping it is adverse to the public interest.*

Arguably, the system Mr. Manning proposes might diminish the effect of advocacy and special-interest groups; certainly, there'd be a tendency for all political ideas to be driven down to a lowest common denominator. But even this isn't true. Special-interest groups would simply be redefined as special-interest groups *with money*. Politicians, working under the threat of "recall," would only be prepared to back measures they felt were "safe," and that would mean "stroking" the electorate and warding off challenges—activities, especially given the importance of

* It should be noted that this isn't Reform's complete program in this area; other measures involve MPs' pensions, the review of contracts and so forth.

the mass media in modern politicking, which only the wealthy could afford. Indeed, all of Mr. Manning's proposals, though justified in terms of transferring power to the people, actually transfer power to money.

A second point to bear in mind is that Mr. Manning is a hinterland politician, and Reform is a western party (including western separatists) trying to capture the whole country under the guise of an ideological conservatism. Mr. Manning's notions, appropriately enough, are very western, in fact western American: to the extent that any of his ideas have contemporary currency, it's in California and the Pacific Northwest. Alberta, as everyone knows, has always had a penchant for the politically eccentric, and it's not unfair to say that just as Mr. Manning's father attempted to foist "funny money" on the country, so his son, with this grab-bag of notions, is attempting to introduce "funny politics" into our national life. Naturally, this sort of thing doesn't come out of Alberta simply because of the water they drink. Alberta is a province of extraordinary ideological conformity; when Peter Lougheed defeated Ernest Manning's successor, Harry Strom, it was simply one set of conservatives replacing another—and exactly the same thing was true when Mr. Klein took over from Mr. Getty. Democracy, then, is not so much exercised through the clash of ideas as through personalities; politics tends to resemble local, municipal politics elsewhere. Indeed, everything in Mr. Manning's "accountability" platform both assumes and encourages this. For example, he would "allow freer voting in the House of Commons." But votes *are* free in the House of Commons; it's just that they take place along party lines. Why? Because the parties represent, or are supposed to represent, ideas and interests whose clash is what

163

politics is all about. But of course this isn't true at the local, municipal level. Disputes about hauling away the snow rarely involve grand ideas, and never coherent systems of ideas—ideologies. To Mr. Manning, coming from Alberta, this is perfectly natural—that's what politics should be, a series of largely *personal* gestures. Indeed, municipal politics is clearly his model. Rather bizarrely, in the "national unity" section of Reform's platform, he promises to "affirm local government as the first level of government closest to the people." It's hard to know what this peculiar statement might mean. Local government, by definition, is the government closest to the people; I don't think many people were aware that this tautology was in need of affirmation. But Mr. Manning is here offering us his model, his ideal. It excludes ideas in any large sense, sees politics as wholly personal, and makes "keeping promises" the crucial political issue. In other words, he takes the discourse of promise to a new and extraordinary extreme.

But this extreme view has other roots in Alberta as well. Albertans, and Westerners generally, are particularly concerned with the forms and processes of "democracy" for a very good reason. They are a minority; and like most minorities, they feel threatened and hard done by—and so are constantly on the lookout for formal, constitutional protections of one sort or another. The parallel with Quebec is obvious. Since their *numbers* leave them without sufficient parliamentary clout—in disputes like that around the National Energy Program, in which Alberta was treated abominably by the federal government—they are always seeking political gadgets and gimmicks to compensate. But such gimmicks, rather than enhancing democracy, always work against it. In Reform's program, you note, the

"Triple E" Senate is revived. Of course this is a dreadful idea. If there's one thing this country doesn't need, it's another level of government. And if there's one thing the city of Ottawa doesn't need, it's another vast encampment of civil servants pushing paper—and don't kid yourself, that's what it would take to feed such a monster. And how would such a Senate be constituted? If it was based on representation by population—democracy, in other words—it would merely place Alberta and the West in a minority position once again. But of course it wouldn't be constituted democratically. The first "E" in Mr. Manning's Senate stands for Equal, which is to say, Alberta would have the same number of seats as Ontario—and that would be clearly undemocratic, the reverse of "accountability."[†]

Ending the Discourse?

That's the key—and the great danger—with these particular notions, and ideas of this general sort. Although they are always justified in terms of democracy, popular control and "closeness to the people," they are not only undemocratic, they are *antidemocratic.* Born out of frustration with the discourse of promise, they appeal to us because they seem to offer a way of bringing that discourse to an end; in fact, rather than ending this particular way of talking and thinking about politics, *they try to end politics altogether,* and replace it with fiat—the law. Sometimes this is easy enough to see. Mr. Manning, for example, periodically muses about a national referendum on abortion. His feelings are

† The solution to this problem is simple enough, at least conceptually. If the western provinces were unified, and represented by a single government, they would have the same clout as Ontario or Quebec. But this is unlikely to happen. The obvious capital of such a western Province would be Saskatoon, and Albertans secretly loathe Saskatooners. On the east coast, antipathy toward Corner Brook creates a similar problem.

strong on this issue; an evangelical Christian, he is, of course, a "right-to-lifer." But how could any referendum produce an outcome more democratic than the one we have today? Under current law, those who want abortions can get them; those who don't are in no way required to have them. If Mr. Manning lost this particular referendum, his side would in fact lose nothing—because no law will force women to abort if they don't want to; but if he won, women who wanted to have abortions would be absolutely denied them.

Such a referendum would be an almost transparent trick. But all referendums are essentially the same. No one, after all, is going to stage a referendum around a question where there is a broad, national consensus. A sharp and close division is an assumption. Inevitably, by a narrow margin—a percentage point or two, perhaps a tenth of one per cent—the will of "the democratic majority" would be forced on the remainder of the population. The winner takes everything—the loser gets nothing. *Formally*, this may represent some philosophic notion of democracy: but it is not democratic *politics*. And it is, even formally, not democratic *parliamentary* politics. Parliamentary democracy exists precisely because it is very dangerous in any civil (and civilized) society, to settle political issues this way. Sharp divisions require leadership, careful thought and compromise—which is why parliamentary legislatures, though elected by the people, are always allowed a degree of independence from the shifting tides of their emotions. But Mr. Manning's politics, his protestations to the country, are actually the most pure development of the discourse of promise, and so tend inevitably to the purely emotional. Through "recall," "citizen initiatives" and referendums—*the tools to ensure that we keep our promises*—he wishes politicians

166

to be tied as closely as possible to those emotions. Officially, within its program, Reform commits itself to only one specific "binding national referendum." Its subject? The return of capital punishment—one of the most violently emotional issues of them all. Which is the point. The inflammation of emotion is what Mr. Manning's politics—the acme of the discourse of promise—seeks out. It replaces ideas with emotion, leadership with personality, debate with demagoguery: again, the discourse of promise carried to the extreme.

And yet there are even more important reasons why referendums are inherently antidemocratic, and one of them will allow me to remind you that Mr. Manning is not alone in his enthusiasm. There is another group, also rooted in the hinterland, with similar violent emotions, which seeks to legitimate itself as "democratic" through the referendum. Of course I mean the separatists. And the two referendums they have held illustrate how false and manipulative referendums almost inevitably are.

The crucial issue, of course, is "the question." Who decides the question the referendum is to be about? And *what* is the question? Here there is an inevitable and insurmountable difficulty, which virtually ensures that any referendum will not be democratic. An issue of sufficient importance to be worthy of a referendum is bound to be complex and difficult, *far too complex and too difficult to be expressed in a simple yes or no question.* That is the absurdity of referendums on "sovereignty" or "independence"—words of vast emotional resonance but little specific content. That is why, in the last Quebec referendum, the "question" was so convoluted and vague—and why an astonishing percentage of Quebecers who voted *oui* expected that they'd still be sending members to a Canadian parliament after a separatist victory. In fact, the point of M. Parizeau's referendum was not "a democratic consultation" but the legitimation of his leadership and anything he chose to do with it: if he'd won, probably a unilateral declaration of Quebec's independence. Supporters of referendums would no doubt blame M. Parizeau, mark him down as an exceptional case—they might point out, for example, that élitism oozes from his every pore. But that won't do. Referendum questions are always set by the power-in-place, and invariably seek to legitimize a course of action already decided upon and embodied in a strong political leader:

> Referenda were introduced as a political tool under the French Revolution, but came into their own under Napoleon. He used them to create something new—a populist dictatorship. Referenda resembled a democratic appeal to the people without requiring the long-term complexities of elected representatives, daily politics, and regular elections. Instead he combined his personal popularity with a highly focused appeal on a single subject. The result was that he could later claim the general support of the populace on any subject for undefined periods of time. In 1804, Napoleon used a referendum to become emperor, thus destroying democracy. Hitler did virtually the same thing in 1933 and 1934. In two referenda he got more power than an absolute monarch.[2]

We don't have to frighten ourselves with names like Hitler, or even Parizeau, to see the truth of this. Virtually all referendums involve a leader's attempt to manipulate the population into accepting a course of action, which, almost by definition is opposed by some significant section of the population.

Democracy *compels* the losing side to accept the "democratic verdict" of the majority as a kind of sentence—which the popular leader will see is carried out. Referendums, then, present themselves as political tools, but they are really tools to end politics. More exactly, they replace politics with the discourse of promise in its most extreme form. Political issues, deprived of their complexity, become reduced to the most simply defined "moral" choices—the religious roots of *promise* begin to flower. And the conduct of politics, under a leader whose own definition would increasingly blur the secular and the theological into the mythological, becomes a series of moral crusades, with promises of almost apocalyptic import.

For the separatists, supposing they should ever win, referendums would come to an end—although, with M. Duceppe, it's hard to be sure. Mr. Manning, on the other hand, would make them a regular part of the system. He would "give voters direct input into decision-making through referendums and citizens' initiatives on important issues." Of course, given the logic of his position, some people might say that this is inevitable. Having sharply reduced party discipline, and with members of parliament working under the threat of "recall," continuous "input" from voters might be the only way to get decisions made.

But this regular appeal to referendums actually highlights something more familiar.

What we have here, again taken to an extreme, is the *fragmentation* and *incoherence* which is such an intrinsic part of the discourse of promise. Politics would lose even the pretence of being a systematic, rational response to history, and become a series of emotionally charged, rhetorically defined plebiscites on particular issues. Confined largely to the media, structured around "campaigns," political debate would become an adjunct to advertising, and the "choices" of citizens would be manipulated in the same way as their "choices" between Pepsi and Coke.

In every way, this is all profoundly conservative. In such a fragmented, incoherent system—with politics broken into an endless series of plebiscites—it becomes impossible to challenge basic assumptions. They are simply never the issue. The general uses and purposes of power are never addressed when political activity is so totally focused on its particular applications. The *status quo* is thus assured. Once more, the connection to local politics—or the politics of Mr. Manning's home province—is evident. In local politics, the uses of power are largely beyond debate; names like Rousseau and Locke are rarely invoked in discussions about carting away snow. The same is true (though not so entirely true) of Alberta. Ralph Klein's success is really based on his asserting a broad, historically derived consensus about the uses of government and power. Mr. Manning shares exactly those assumptions. And part of his current success is because, at least briefly, something of the same historical conditions have created a similar national consensus. Extreme anxiety about the economy and people's own economic situations, a genuine (and reasonable) distress about the fiscal situation of Canadian governments and a fundamental worry about the country's very future given Quebec separatism—all part of the collapse of "the big promise"—have combined to push people into a basic, minimalist notion of government: "common sense" rules everywhere, not just in Ontario.

But Mr. Manning's system is extraordinarily conservative in another way as well. With systematic, programmatic political thinking abolished, with rationality of any kind marginalized, only one element can hold it together, The Leader. Already, this tendency is well enough illustrated in the history of the separatists; as their "thought" has gradually dissolved—moving from "independence" to "sovereignty association" to M. Duceppe's nebulous "partnership"—the meaning of their politics has been absorbed, and is now almost wholly expressed, in the personality of The Leader, currently M. Bouchard. *Promise* uses faith, belief and hope to bridge the gulf between the governed and The Leader; taken to this extreme, the population now entrusts itself totally to a leader defined in purely emotional, and increasingly mythological and theological terms.

And so despite our frustration with *promise*, we helplessly reproduce it, in a debased but intensified form; seeking to escape a swamp, we wade deeper into it. Up to now, *promise* has existed as a discourse, a peculiar language we have tried to use to talk about politics. But this language has been ill-defined, its vocabulary evolving gradually, its grammar taking shape over years. With the politics of people like Preston Manning, what we're really seeing is *the systematization of promise*. It is being solidified into a concrete set of rules and procedures, within which "politics" would be confined. In effect, and quite appropriately, this is an extension of the *cut government* theme which is so important to politicians of this sort—for "politics" is here cut back to a stump. Basic issues of power cannot be addressed. Political ideas are transformed into sentiments of a vaguely religious type. And political debate becomes a purely emotional and symbolic contest conducted under a leadership whose formal abasement to the will of a fragmented, manipulated population shapes a defining omnipotence.

Associating these final developments with Mr. Manning's name may create the impression that all this is somehow a project of "the right." But that is a trap. Mr. Manning may be using and shaping the discourse of promise to his own, particular ends, but he is entirely consistent with *promise* itself. He is simply following, to its ultimate conclusion, a discourse which has happily shaped the "left" for two generations. A hinterland politician, his political identity defined by federal-provincial conflicts, who conducts politics by targeting and dividing the voters, and defines his leadership around trust and moral righteousness, he is as Canadian as . . . Audrey McLaughlin, or Lloyd Axworthy or Sheila Copps or . . . but you can fill in the blanks for yourself. Fundamentally, they are all much the same—for the only language they know is the language of *promise*.

Chapter Eight

—<o>—

Promises, Polls
and Prospects

*B*y happy coincidence—an appropriate conjunction of the literary and political—the main text of the essay you've just read was completed on the first of June, 1997, and handed over to FedEx, for delivery to my publishers, on June second: the day we Canadians once more rolled our eyes and elected another parliament.

In my own riding, I should note, voting is a purely formal exercise. The constituency of Ottawa-Vanier—which includes the prime minister's residence and Rideau Hall—has returned a Liberal in every election since Confederation, and there was no reason to think that this time might be any different. Still, feeling full of virtue at having completed a job of work, I decided I might as well vote. I live in Lower Town. This is the heart of the old French-speaking section of the city—though it may offend M. Bouchard's ear, *joual* means home to me. Appropriately, my polling station was in the francophone community centre, or Patro—from *patronale*, any building or person associated with a patron saint—and I waited quietly as three nuns did their duty by God, the bishop and—you may be sure—the Liberal Party. Then I made my X, deposited my ballot, and headed for the links. That evening, watching the results come in, I thought of those nuns again, for the Liberals certainly must have had God on their side, certainly in Ontari-ari-ari-o. They swept the province. The sole Reformer was driven out—and the Reform vote significantly cut—while the Tory heart of the Queen's old province was reduced to a single beat, in Markham.

At the same time, it was clear that the battle of election day had been a near-run thing: a bare majority for the Liberals, with Tory gains in the Maritimes and Quebec, a quiet success for the NDP, Reform solid in the West. What had happened? The Liberals, after all, hadn't called this election to *barely* win.

In truth, nothing had gone right for the Liberals. The election call itself had been a disaster, a slow-moving unravelling of the inevitable rather than anything decisive. But when the vote was finally called, southern Manitoba was underwater, Winnipeg threatened, our first western province physically and emotionally exhausted. Did these people want to listen to the blatherings of federal politicians? Perhaps not. But did the Liberals care? Not when they could smell a big majority in the polls. So they went ahead anyway—the plans of God, Mother Nature and Gaia couldn't stand in the way of truly important things.

Arrogant? Of course. Typically, the Liberals seemed genuinely surprised at the reaction of the country. By way of damage control, they dispatched Charles Kingsley, the Chief Electoral Officer, to pronounce his blessing on the whole proceeding. Of course he did—but then he didn't care much about the West either, in fact *he didn't even know what time it was in Saskatchewan.* So the people in the heart of the Canadian prairie, whose wheat remains one of the enduring symbols of this country, didn't quite vote along with the rest of us. All this could be called merely symbolic, but not if you were a Liberal candidate in the West in 1997.

Down East—where the vote provided the first surprise of election night—the situation was a little different. Cuts to social services and unemployment insurance truly hurt the Maritimes. Liberal candidates knew this, but going into an election in which everyone was expecting a big Liberal win, they thought they had the answer: *Vote for us or there'll be no patronage.* Maritimers, as we all know, are past masters when it comes to patronage, but they don't like being bullied. And the Liberals bullied. It was their whole strategy. But in the Maritimes, where Reform has scarcely penetrated, the Tory machine could still get out the vote; and the NDP, running with a local lady as their leader—she turned in a nervous, gritty performance, like a grade-school teacher facing her first day of class—gave a real account of themselves. The heads of ministers rolled.

For the Liberals, this was bad enough. But there was also Jean Charest. Decisively winning the debates, campaigning effectively and energetically, he'd started a strong Tory current running in Quebec. If this had spilled across the border—if voters in Quebec had begun to believe in a Tory revival in Ontario—it could have become a tide; which would, precisely, have raised the Tories' hope in Ontario by suggesting that there might be a national alternative to the Libs. So the Liberals pulled out all the stops. In the media, especially the CBC—Jim Coutts's old baili-wick—the order went out, *get Charest.* Reporters obediently began doing stories on the Tories' weak organization in Quebec, while Quebec voters were told that M. Charest wasn't making it among *les Anglais.* In an interview with M. Charest, Hana

Gartner came on like the First Lady of Reform. And, in general, when they weren't attacking him, they did their best to ignore him. And finally, to make extra sure, in the last week of the campaign, the prime minister stated that fifty per cent plus one would not be enough to win a future referendum; that drove enough of the Quebec nationalist vote away from the Tories, and back to the Bloc, to hold the Conservative surge in Quebec to a modest size. So Jean Charest was cheated. But he did well enough. Perhaps, as a general judgment on the whole affair, you could say that they all did *well enough*. The Liberals hung on to government. The Tories stepped back from the brink of extinction, while proving they had the best leader in the country. The NDP revived themselves. The Bloc, though trimmed, was still large enough to be a force in Ottawa. And Reform, decisively driven out of Ontario and reduced to a western clique, nonetheless could claim the title of Official Opposition.

But what of *promise*?

The obvious place to begin answering this question is with the campaigns, the *locus classicus* of the whole discourse. In their different ways, they were all quite interesting, the minor campaigns —the Bloc and the NDP—perhaps especially so. So far as *promise* is concerned, M. Duceppe's efforts for the Bloc Québécois illustrate clearly how "ideas," defined in this discourse, very quickly lose force: they come to exist almost solely on the emotional and symbolic plane, embodied in The Leader. *Politics becomes nothing but leadership, and leadership becomes nothing but personality.* Obviously, by this measure, the Bloc was in trouble from the start; personality-wise, M. Duceppe was distinctly lacking. Still, I came to feel a certain sympathy for him as he bumbled along. Losing his dignity most mornings, he usually managed to recover by evening: he proves that sincerity is not a great virtue, but a virtue nonetheless. The trouble is, his sincerity compels him to take separatism seriously, as an *idea,* and it is one of the silliest ideas around. So he was continuously attempting to explain the inexplicable, rationalize the irrational—moving from the vacuousness of "partnership" to the absurdity of a revolving-door referendum: he actually suggested that Quebec, having voted to leave Canada, would be free to vote itself back in. Most especially, he was utterly unable to deal with the logic of the partition of Quebec. And this is not only logical, it is inevitable, as the history of this century amply proves; almost all the ethnic European states, products of Wilsonian democracy after the First World War, have fractured into smaller and smaller units. The human animal (being what it is) has produced a history in which no state is ethnically "clean," and the various ethnicities within Quebec—the English, the polyglot mongrels of Montreal, various Indian groups, the peculiar, unpronounceable enclave we in the *Outaouais* form—have as much call on "democracy" as anyone else. So, predictably, M. Duceppe had to be rescued. Smiling benignly, stuffed into a new waistcoat, Jacques Parizeau was waddled out. M. Bouchard appeared as well, but Mr. Parizeau was probably more important, and that was significant. Jacques Parizeau has a certain mythological role within separatism, embodying the notion that it might, somewhere, contain a genuine idea; and of course this was M. Duceppe's particular problem—on the intellectual plane, he revealed how silly separatism was. M. Parizeau, temporarily reinstated as Leader, was effective, or effective enough.

With the Liberals' help, and a final boost from Mr. Manning, the Bloc managed respectability.

Promises, Promises

As for the NDP, their campaign was entirely nostalgic, reaching back to their roots as "the conscience of the country"—they made an explicit appeal to their origins in the social gospel. And since their leader, according to *Frank* magazine (usually reliable in such matters) was engaged in a love affair with a decent, well-meaning man of the cloth, this couldn't have been more appropriate. But I don't want to sound facetious. The NDP's goal, expressed negatively, was to avoid extinction; positively, to achieve official party status in the Commons. *Nostalgia*, therefore, was a deliberate strategic choice, and an intelligent one. Rather than advancing, and convincing people about a program which everyone knew they would never be able to implement, they wanted to define themselves as a necessary political force. This, inevitably, evoked their peculiar religious past, and that of course is inextricably bound up with *promise*. But it's important to remember that the religious roots of the NDP are also distinct from *promise*, and are part of a Protestant tradition that has fed social democratic parties everywhere. *Promise*, indeed, has allowed that tradition to be secularized, and to become instrumental—even if the Liberals, largely, have actually done it. In fact, a large part of the NDP's role in the country, certainly since the seventies, has been, precisely, the legitimization of this form of political discourse. They have been especially important in legitimating the shift away from a view of government whose relations to the population are rooted in a conception of a common citizenship to one in which government relates to people in terms of special needs (victimization) or identity—the *frag-mentation* of the population, which is so important to *promise*. Since the triumph of *promise* (or this aspect of it) has opened universal social programs to attack, the NDP's role as "defender" of these programs is decidedly hypocritical. But then, no doubt, hypocrisy is especially familiar to religious people; they know how to carry it off. Alexa McDonough certainly did. Most of the time, as mentioned, she was reminiscent of a school teacher, but at news conferences, standing behind a lectern, one thought of pulpits and heard the echo of choirs behind her. Eschewing power, she called us to something Higher. Her programmatic pronouncements, such as they were, stressed that grand old Christian theme, full of the glory of salvation—tax the rich and give to the poor. Trapped in the discourse of promise, now without any other way to think, the NDP, rather ironically, doesn't have much to promise *except themselves*.

Again, however, this worked *well enough*. To the NDP's particular credit, they not only accomplished their minimal goal—achieving official party status—but also managed something which Reform, or Social Credit before it, couldn't manage: although not a national party, because they have no standing in Quebec, they have now broken completely with their hinterland past. On the other hand, the NDP's appeal is without focus, grounded in sentimentality rather than ideology, or anything more concrete. For some people, supporting the NDP will always be satisfactory. They not only feel good, they feel Good. For such people, *promise* is not only their political discourse, it forms the basis for all their discourse: they embrace this way of looking at the world more completely than anyone else. A week after the election, Stanley Knowles, one of the old social gospellers, passed away. I only met Stanley Knowles a couple of times—he reminded me of a minor character in some book by Dickens. But when he first came to Ottawa as a young MP, he'd needed a place to live, and with his frugal heart, he took a room in the house of a man named Wally Mann, who eventually taught me English at Lisgar Collegiate. Walter Mann and his wife, Marjorie, were both rare people, truly dedicated to the art of teaching (any infelicities in these pages are not to be laid at that particular door) and of course ardent social democrats. In any case, I was astonished to learn that when Knowles died he was still living there; he never moved—not in all the years he was in Ottawa. But then, I suppose, why would he? The room would have been clean and dry, the conversation always congenial and, when required, elevated. I gather he was too ill, at the end, to follow the election, which is a little sad. He would have recognized, in the NDP, the same old party, gospelling along—and perhaps (beloved word!) even making a little progress.

Turning to the Conservatives, we can see the fate of *promise* as it has been worked out, both in Canada and the United States, on the right of the political spectrum. The campaign of Mike Harris in Ontario was central to this. Interestingly, in the Clinton-Dole campaign of 1996, the Republicans frequently referred to Mr. Harris's campaign as a model. At the centre of the Dole campaign, recall, was the proposal for a massive tax cut; when this didn't immediately strike a chord with the electorate, right-wing tacticians and commentators pressed Dole not to give up on it, pointing out that Mr. Harris, with a similar sort of promise, had come from well behind to win.

This was the sort of thinking that lay behind the Conservative campaign of 1997—although they had clearly learned nothing from Dole's failure. Indeed, in making their proposal for a cut in income taxes, the Conservatives made a fatal political error: *believing your own rhetoric.* Mr. Harris had *not* won because of his tax-cut proposal, or at least that had only been one small element in a very complex victory. Most important, the Harris tax cut, as well as his whole program, was played off the record and stance of the Rae government. The Liberal government at the federal level was scarcely that: Paul Martin had, in reality, cut a good deal out of federal expenditures, and represented himself as having cut a good deal more. Besides, by that point, the country had the experience of people like Klein and Harris to reflect upon. Tax cuts and spending cuts were inextricably linked in the public mind—as indeed they should have been. And provincial spending cuts had reached the point where they were genuinely disturbing people, in every part of the political spectrum. Even the supporters of Klein and Harris probably hesitated at the prospect of a Harris-style government at the federal level. One such government was enough.

But even more important to the failure of the Conservative proposal was the reason it had failed for Dole. *Promise*, as we've seen, always displaces content, the programmatic. Party programs, and the individual promises that make them up, are no longer evaluated with any kind of critical sense—in regard, say, to what they might actually accomplish. We say "politicians never keep their promises," and pretend that we don't expect them to, but this only expresses our anger that they don't, our hope that they will. We *want* to believe, and above all we want to believe in the system, the whole discourse, since it ultimately promises *that everything will be all right.* Increasingly, individual promises are subordinate to this more general purpose, and have a more purely formal role, that is, affirming the system of which they are a part: for the population, sustaining their belief in "the big promise," for the politician, defining him as trustworthy. Because of this, large-scale programmatic efforts embodied in large promises are risky for democratic politicians today; in general, you're better off promising less, using individual promises to target particular groups within a fragmented electorate, and defining the political leader in sentimental terms, surrounding him with a "feel-good" aura. (This is why almost all successful political promises, made to an increasingly infantile electorate, involve some sort of appeal around children.) Accordingly, the promise of a big tax cut was unlikely to succeed, as Dole discovered. And this was doubly true in Canada. After years of being told (especially by Conservatives) that the nation's finances were in peril, the idea of such a tax cut was too much to swallow. Moreover, *not* believing the Conservatives became a way of punishing them, a way of asserting resentment against Mulroney and the economic anxiety associated with him. So the Liberals ran ads that said the Conservatives' numbers didn't add up, and were almost universally believed. The *facts*, of course, were something else. Insofar as they ever do, the Conservatives' numbers probably did add up, and their tax-cut proposal, I'm prepared to bet, will be implemented by the Liberals in the next few years. But facts, as we've seen, have little to do with *promise*. The discourse of promise is about faith and belief, and these emotions—around the Conservatives and tax cuts—were in short supply. Parties of the right often like to feel that they don't participate in the discourse of promise, but that's because they

184

only see certain aspects of it. In fact, they're mired in it; the whole Conservative program, both in content and language, was an old-fashioned exercise in *promise*—federal-provincial relations are actually called "A Canadian Covenant" in their platform document—and it simply didn't fly.

The tax-cut proposal almost finished the Conservatives; it allowed "responsible" opinion to dismiss them, virtually out of hand. But, as everyone knows, M. Charest rescued himself in the debates. He won the debates (both in English and French) for three reasons. The first, although not relevant to this discussion, is worth noting—he was the best debater; lively, articulate, able to think on his feet, he virtually chaired the proceedings, taking them over so completely that one was almost embarrassed for his colleagues on the platform. The second reason was his *modernity*. M. Charest is younger than all the other national political leaders; more importantly, however, he is the only one of them who actually seems to be living in the last years of the twentieth century. Chrétien is living in 1963; Mr. Manning in 1953; Alexa McDonough in 1933; and the separatists barely make it into this century—or at least their sort of mysticism should have died with Charles Péguy on the Marne. In short, M. Charest was the only one of the leaders with whom people could identify, *believe* in—here, he did find grounds for faith. And he then exploited this by saying something people wanted to believe, when he delivered a straightforward, passionate pitch for a united Canada. In this, he didn't actually use the word "promise"; rather, he spoke of a "commitment" to his children. No matter. Here, for the only time in the campaign, a major candidate successfully mobilized the discourse of promise in a positive way. Its believability was embodied in M. Charest's persona as a young, modern Québécois; its patriotism mobilized powerful emotions and a great ideal; and it was unencumbered by any serious intellectual content: the only idea M. Charest had to offer was an eviscerated version of "distinct society." But that was enough for his purposes. In polls, he was already ahead of his competitors in personal popularity; by the end of the campaign, by a wide margin, he was identified as the best potential prime minister. Energized, his campaign now took off, especially in Quebec, and only desperate manoeuvring by the Liberals kept it in check.

Of all the parties, Reform defined its campaign most completely in terms of *promise*. But in a very particular way—which is appropriate enough, because Reform is different from the other parties, with the possible exception of the Bloc. In fact, like the Bloc, it's only a political party in the formal sense of the word. It's more of a movement, or at least the tag end of one, the mobilization of a western political alienation that feeds itself from a variety of forces: disaffected Conservatism, Social Credit and the separatism of entities like the Western Canada Concept Party. It's also the personal political vehicle of Preston Manning, identified and defined by his leadership in a way different from all other parties. So, although presenting itself in the guise of a "national" party, in reality it seeks the redefinition of the nation along western lines, peculiar to Mr. Manning. In this sense—as a hinterland movement—it's almost a pure expression of the discourse of promise, offering the vision of a new covenant, only vaguely defined, but harnessing the most powerful of emotions, rooted in a past that evokes the mythologized childhood of its

Promises, Promises

supporters. Reflecting the importance of evangelical Christianity in the West and Mr. Manning's personal religious beliefs, the party's "program" and the language which expresses it are saturated with a religiosity which, as we have seen, defines one whole side of *promise*.

You'll note that I've put "program" in quotation marks—because, in reality, Reform's program is a sham. It has to be—you can't put forward a national program when you don't believe in the nation itself, only a single part of it. Accordingly, as you read through their election documents—and as Mr. Manning spoke throughout the campaign—they engendered a distinct sense of unreality. Mr. Manning didn't quite sound crazy, though in his leather jacket he certainly looked a little wild; but he didn't seem to be living in the same world as the rest of us. *Promise*, of course, is only concerned with reality in a very particular way; but there's usually some reference to it. With Reform, this is reaching the vanishing point, the "reality" referred to being almost wholly a creation of Reform itself, a pure fantasy. Their proposals around crime illustrate this well enough. The only piece of Reform campaign literature that came through my letter box was about crime, and seemed to imply that the country had been engulfed by a vast eruption of criminal activity. The trouble was, on that same day, *The Ottawa Sun*—not known as an organ of liberal opinion—was headlined "Cops Cuff Crime"; that is to say, crime, at least in the capital, was a declining problem, as proved by police statistics. In the same way, when Mr. Manning promises that a Reform government would "Enact a *Victims' Bill of Rights* that puts the rights of law-abiding Canadians ahead of those of criminals," the Canada to which he is referring can exist only in his imagination. In the real Canada, all citizens are equal before the law, certainly the criminal law; those who break it do not obtain rights "ahead of" victims, or anybody else. Most of Mr. Manning's "program" had this quality; it invented a fictitious country and gave it largely fictitious problems to justify proposals that would allow him to mobilize emotions, and largely *negative* emotions—fear and anger. But this created a difficulty. *Promise* plays to emotions, as Reform did, and prefers them to be extreme emotions, even tending toward the apocalyptic—and Mr. Manning proved skilful enough at this. But, tactically, the point is to target particular sections of the population and use differing promises with different appeals to connect with them. Reform's program simply made the same appeal, in the same way, to the same target audience, over and over. And although that audience may have been substantial in the West, it was just not large enough to form the basis for national electoral success.

By the last week or so of the campaign, this was becoming very apparent in the polls. Most especially, Reform's campaign was not working in Ontario, which had to be the basis for any extension of Reform from its western, hinterland base. At this point, Reform's true program was unveiled, in the form of an ad directed against leading politicians from Quebec—Messrs Chrétien, Charest, Duceppe, etc. As one American commentator, writing in *The International Herald Tribune*, expressed it, here was "the ferocity of Preston Manning,"[1] for this ad couldn't have been uglier. Grainy, black-and-white mugshots of politicians born in Quebec were plastered over with the universal sign for "no entry." In stark terms, Mr. Manning had revealed his vision of the country. Failing to conquer its metropolitan centres, Mr. Manning, as a hinterland politician, simply chose to define them out. In Ontario—the crucial battleground for Mr. Manning, and everyone else—it was a clarion call to the small-town, Protestant, anti-French province that existed in the days of Manning *père*, and even in Mr. Manning's own childhood: that golden era when French Canadians knew their place, and cereal boxes weren't cluttered with their peculiar language. And that Ontario still exists, out in the boondocks. But Ontario is now Metropolitan Toronto, the Golden Horseshoe—even Ottawa's population has reached a million. Manning's crude anti-French appeal simply didn't work. In Ontario, the Reform vote dropped, and they lost their only seat.

In a sense, by revealing the true nature of Reform's program—a Canada that excluded Quebec—Mr. Manning was only being true to the promise that forms the core of his hinterland politics. It sees the future in terms of a mythical past, indeed just as separatism in Quebec tries to do. It projects onto the whole country the culture of a single part of it: the conservative, rural values of small-town Alberta are to be the national ideal, the Promised Land, an English-speaking equivalent to M. Bouchard's Kingdom of the Saguenay.

Moreover, Reform's program in this respect is also true to Mr. Manning as a political personality. Pierre Trudeau was elected prime minister almost thirty years ago, but Mr. Manning apparently doesn't speak enough French to order dinner, let alone carry on a political debate. That, let's not kid ourselves, represents a political choice. To be a good Canadian, you must be able to speak *either* English *or* French. But the prime minister's job, like all jobs, has qualifications. In a country in which French is an official language, in which one-quarter of the population speaks it as their mother tongue, in a country afflicted with a major secessionist movement amongst its French-speaking citizens—in such a country, speaking the language of Molière, or at least John Diefenbaker, is an essential requirement. Mr. Manning's failure here is telling. He is not qualified to be prime minister *unless and until Quebec is driven from the country*, and that is the real promise which his politics makes, and seeks to keep.*

With the Liberals, I am faced with a difficulty. Normally, if you're a writer and you wish to describe something, you can count on reality to offer some organizing principle, some element of coherence. I don't mean anything complex by this. If you're describing a person, for example, you usually start at the head and work down—the human body organizes itself that way. Or think of a landscape, foreground and background—the stark silhouette of a thorn tree, the long dun sweep of a heat-soaked plain, and then, far-off, glistening, the shining peak of Kilimanjaro. You take my point. Even complex human events, like war, usually offer something—causes, battle plans, rival generals, the first shots, so forth. But the Liberal campaign of 1997? There's nothing, no rhyme, no reason, no pattern whatsoever. Language itself, syntax, imposes an order that wasn't there. It was a total mess. Only a chimpanzee, randomly pecking at a keyboard, could adequately describe it. Mr. Chrétien had nothing to say, and said it badly. Jetting back and forth across the

* I saw no Reform campaign literature in French. On the Internet, their Web site had no French pages. Of course this is consistent with their program, which seeks the abolition of official bilingualism. By contrast, the Bloc Québécois provided an English-language service on their Web site.

country, he always landed in the same state of confusion. He showed up—I suppose you can say that much. And although he sometimes forgot the names of his candidates, he always seems to have recalled his own: an achievement, by his standards. Of course, the people organizing this were the same lot that had almost lost the referendum—their incompetence was tried, tested and true. Well ahead when the campaign began, they once more eked out a victory.

Promise played into this in three particular ways. On election night, commenting on the results, Preston Manning said, "This is what happens when a government breaks its promises." And the broken promises of the Liberals had put them on the defensive from the very opening of the campaign. Actually, it was worse than this. Although they were continuously nagged about broken promises—especially the GST—the attacks against the Liberals never really crystallized around this issue, or at least not in such a way that the Liberals could face it down. That is, even before the campaign began, they were already so tarred with this particular brush that they could never recover. Indeed, in an Environics poll released on April 1, 74 per cent indicated unhappiness with the Liberals on "promise keeping" while only 14 per cent said they'd done a good job. Even among Liberal supporters, the negative margin was very high. This failure drastically limited M. Chrétien's leadership appeal. As late as the televised debates, he was still saying that "we never did what we wanted on the GST," rather than straightforwardly apologizing—he could simply never bring himself to do it. So his strong suit as a campaigner—his "ordinary joe" appeal—was unavailable to him.

But the broken promises of the Liberals hurt them in another way as well—they couldn't make any *new* promises. Of course, they tried to take the high road here: they weren't making promises, they claimed, because they were "responsible," concerned about the deficit. But they would have been much better off following Clinton's approach in his campaign against Dole; paying due regard to the need for fiscal responsibility, but offering a variety of small, particular promises with a sentimental "feel good" appeal. But M. Chrétien's credibility had been so weakened around the GST that he couldn't even manage that. This failure then played into another negative. The Liberals, only three years into their mandate, had no "issue" to campaign on—so their failure to offer even a simple menu of promises meant their campaign had virtually no positive thrust at all.

But, in any case, the Liberals were running on their record. As a practical matter, that record was the implementation of Brian Mulroney's economic program—spending cuts, increasing revenue (the GST, among other taxes), a tremendous growth in exports (NAFTA), all leading to a balanced budget. In fact, the success of those policies constitutes a major vindication of Mr. Mulroney's politics, or at least the economic side of it. Obviously, the Liberals couldn't admit this. So their whole program, as previously discussed, was wrapped in a peculiar, anachronistic, nostalgic garb in which Mr. Chrétien, the little guy from Shawinigan, became an updated version of Uncle Louis St. Laurent. This had worked quite well in the previous campaign and in government. To a degree, it fitted Mr. Chrétien's personal style; it was in accord with his philosophy of government; and it appealed to the public, because it harked back to the great Liberal governments of the fifties and sixties, when "the big promise" was still viable. Striving to fit this image, Mr. Chrétien's government had presented itself as competent, honest, prudent—*reassuring*. And it had done a reasonably good job of this. In contrast, for example, to the Rae government (or, in a different way, Mike Harris's), it managed to cut government spending without engendering a sense of crisis. But, transferred to an election campaign, there were two difficulties here. Recalling "the big promise" was one thing; actually making it an integral part of Liberal strategy was quite another. The population certainly *wanted* to believe that promise; but that is some distance from belief itself. In the statistics, the "recovery" was impressive; but it still wasn't real in the streets—high unemployment and stagnant personal incomes had left the population demoralized and insecure. And Mr. Chrétien's faltering personal performance—around the GST and the referendum—meant that he hadn't lived up to the myth he was trying to re-create. Moreover, the *competent* centre of the government wasn't Mr. Chrétien, but Paul Martin. In government, this was fine. Mr. Martin's own family tree actually helped, since his father had been such an integral part of the Liberals' glory days; and to say that Mr. Martin, as finance minister, was doing a fair imitation of Walter Harris would be unfair to him—working under much more difficult circumstances, he was actually a good deal better. But finance ministers aren't the centre of election campaigns. Although the Liberals did their best to make use of Mr. Martin, it was Mr. Chrétien who had to carry the ball, and he fumbled it continuously. Mr. Chrétien's failure as a campaigner then redounded on itself. Rather than a sure, well-organized progress—a competent march to victory—the Liberal campaign quickly began to reflect uncertainty and insecurity (much as their referendum campaign had done), so that the memory of the "big promise" faded completely. If Louis St. Laurent was recalled, it was in his dreadful, final campaign of 1957.

For the Liberals, their situation created a fine irony. No party had made greater use of the discourse of promise; they couldn't function without it. "Policy," to people like Chaviva Hosek—the prime minister's policy adviser—was inconceivable in any other terms. Going right back to the days of "multiculturalism," the Liberal Party has used the power of the federal government to attack Canadian citizenship at every turn, expending enormous sums to divide us by race, language, region, sex and every other available principle. Jean Chrétien, from his days as minister of Indian affairs, has been intimately involved in this. But now, because of the peculiar tactical situation that confronted the Liberals, the discourse of promise was largely unavailable to them. Of course, since they knew nothing else, they tried to use it anyway. The most pitiful example was the prime minister's appointment, over the heads of constituency associations, of a number of women candidates, all in the name of "equality"—the rough-and-tumble of contemporary politics was apparently too much for certain lady politicians, who required "affirmative action" to continue their careers. But this sordid exercise in cronyism merely highlighted how much was missing. There was no content to the Liberal campaign, only form. For years, the strategy and tactics of the Liberal Party of Canada had been dictated by the discourse of promise. They had become past masters at fragmenting the country, then, at election time, assembling the pieces—this, to the Liberals, is what "national party" means. In government, they had long since ceased to respond to national needs, preferring to use the power of the bureaucracy to magnify, and build upon, division—immensely skilled at this, they had in consequence created a country divided in a thousand ways, ruled by a bureaucracy of unprecedented scope and size. Inevitably, however, they had forgotten what the nation was; in the referendum campaign, the prime minister had almost lost it, and in this election he certainly didn't find it again. Worse, from an electoral point of view, the only sure base of power for the Liberals was in the bureaucracy itself. The discourse of promise, as exemplified in the Liberal Party, appeared exhausted in 1997. If the campaign had gone on another week, the Liberals might have lost their government, and the prime minister his parliamentary seat.

II

In a sense, nothing demonstrates the triumph of *promise* more completely than the Liberals' failure; deprived of it, they went nowhere, despite beginning with a substantial lead. But they were only "deprived" of *promise* because of special circumstances and in particular ways; it didn't indicate that they wanted to make politics in any other way, nor that the electorate was seeking something else. If anything, the opposite was true. The Liberals were slapped on the wrist for "breaking" promises, and reminded of the discourse which has been so central to their power: in voting against them, people weren't rejecting that system but registering their anger at the possibility it might not continue. They didn't want "cuts"—they wanted "goodies." They wanted someone to make *everything all right.* So the discourse of promise shaped the Liberal campaign, and the campaigns of all the other parties. *Promise*, now the dominant form of political discourse, shaped the country and would shape the future. What did the country look like? What would the future be?

Waking up on June the third, the answer seemed clear enough—editorialists, pundits, all of television's commentators agreed that the country was now divided as it had never been before. Virtually every Canadian source expressed this view, but on the principle that it's often useful to see ourselves as others see us, here is the analysis of Charles Krauthammer, who writes for *The Washington Post* and *The International Herald Tribune*:

Last Monday, Canada held a national election. The results show a country in an advanced state of fracture.

Canada used to have three major parties. They represented different ideologies. There was a party of the left (the New Democratic Party), the center (the Liberals) and the right (the Progressive Conservatives).

No longer. The NDP and the PC were effectively wiped out in the 1993 Parliamentary elections and have only made feeble comebacks.

What is left?

There are still three major parties. But they are regional and ethnic. The Liberal Party has survived and, with a bare majority in the new Parliament, remains the ruling party. But it did so by winning two-thirds of all its seats in one province, Ontario. (Canada has 10.) In Ontario, the Liberals won 101 of 103 seats.

Ontario is the geographic and economic center of Canada. To one side is Quebec; to the other, the West. In Quebec, the majority of seats was won by a radically ethnic and separatist party, the Bloc Québécois. Its platform is the separation of Quebec from Canada. It sends its delegation to the national Parliament in Ottawa for the principal purpose of breaking up the country.

To the other side of Ontario are the Western (prairie) provinces stretching all the way to the Pacific. The Reform Party, the second-largest party in Parliament and now the official opposition, swept 70 percent of the seats in the West. It won not a single seat anywhere else in Canada.

The Reform Party does talk about lower taxes and less government, standard conservative fare. But its real attraction is that it is anti-Quebec. The establishment, it charges, has been trying to keep Canada together with too many concessions to Quebec.

The soft Easterners would give Quebec the status of a "Distinct Society" within Canada and extraordinary control over its language, culture, immigration and other functions. Reform rejects special status. Its platform is equality for all the provinces—read: Get Quebec off its pedestal—and if Quebec doesn't like it, it can go jump in the Atlantic.

On Monday, the Liberals won. Ontario—bland, reasonable, accommodating—rules. For now. But the Reform Party will rail and Quebec will soon have another one of its referenda.

The separatists have lost twice. But they lost the last one by less than one percent. And they vow to keep holding them until they win, at which point Canada will indeed collapse. The next referendum is probably less than two years away . . .[2]

Mr. Krauthammer continues, drawing lessons from the Canadian experience for his American audience, but let me leave it there; his analysis, in some ways, may be a little simple, but it has a great virtue—he keeps his eye on the ball. Most especially, he stresses the three obvious points that defined the election result—the regionalism, which everyone has commented on; the particular importance of the Bloc and Reform; and the position of Ontario. Bearing what he says in mind, let's see if our understanding of the discourse of promise allows us to get a little closer to the truth.

To begin, all analyses of the election result stressed *regionalism*, but this is only a descriptive term—and not a very accurate one—and barely works as a starting point for analysis. The success of Reform and the Bloc represents the success, not of regional politics, but of *hinterland* politics, a particular aspect of *promise*. Canada's history and geography—and its economy—have created regions; but the politics that comes out of those regions has been defined in a very particular way. We usually forget this. "Regionalism" is now such a fundamental part of our politics that we assume it must have the form that it does, but there's nothing inevitable about this at all. Other countries have regions, too—but they shape their politics quite differently. In Canada, regional aspirations and grievances have been defined within the broader discourse of promise, a political discourse which has legitimated, generally, a politics of fragmentation, incoherence and extreme emotionalism—so extreme that it always flirts with the millennial and apocalyptic, endlessly searching for a new covenant. In the particular cases of the Bloc and Reform, both define themselves by projecting very particular hinterland values onto the country as a whole, and against the values of *la métropole*—defined, in both cases, as a cosmopolitan, multilingual, urban and ethnically diverse centre (Montreal/Canada for the Bloc; Toronto/"the East" for Reform). Note that I say *values*. Since there is a vague ideological tradition in our politics (which *promise* has now largely displaced) both these political formations do attempt a crude rationalization of their positions. In the case of Reform—to use Mr. Krauthammer's words—this gives us Mr. Manning's *standard conservative fare.* And, with the separatists, we have the notion of ethnic statehood, a notion rooted in nineteenth-century romanticism and (disastrously) the Wilsonian idealism of Versailles. But these "ideas" continuously dissolve, revealing the true *feelings* and values beneath them. Mr. Manning produces endless briefing papers and "model budgets," but his real program is anti-abortion, abolishing bilingualism and bringing back capital punishment. And once you get a couple of drinks into Mr. Parizeau, he'll start babbling about "the ethnics" and reveal the true basis of his position. The "programs" of both these groups are actually "visions," *promises* of salvation—whose content, such as it is, is wholly nostalgic, as appealing as the rosiest memories of a happy childhood in which every promise is faithfully kept. Mr. Manning wants to carry us back to an imaginary world in the fifties, before divorce, abortion, bilingualism and pot—Messrs Parizeau, Duceppe and Bouchard wish to transport Quebec back to much the same place, a unilingual heaven where women had enough babies to protect *la race blanche* and ethnicity was no more threatening than chicken chow mein. In all this, the Bloc has a slight advantage. The intelligentsia of Montreal, naturally and inevitably, is defined by the French language: they feel the minority status of Quebec particularly acutely. Otherwise, the possibility of living in a country over which Yves Duceppe had any influence whatsoever would give Lise Bissonnette nightmares, and she'd be striving mightily to confine his political ambitions to La Societé Saint-Jean-Baptiste—where his sort of eschatology properly belongs. Mr. Manning, by contrast, has far fewer allies within *la métropole*. Some, like David Frum, are prepared to turn a blind eye to the real heart of Mr. Manning's platform and ambitions, defining him purely in neo-conservative terms. But this is a difficult leap of faith; besides, as a basis of loyalty, it's much more uncertain.

With this in mind, the "regionalism" of the election result becomes somewhat more complex than most people have assumed.

Obviously, the Bloc was confined to Quebec, Reform to the West. But it's noteworthy that Reform, *even in its western base,* remains a largely rural and small-town political expression. The Liberals or NDP won seats or ran strongly in Winnipeg, Regina, Saskatoon, Edmonton and Vancouver. Ralph Klein and Gary Filmon—the premiers of Alberta and Manitoba—both supported the Conservatives, if only for local reasons. And the seat total for Reform barely edged up. In other words, although Reform has been tremendously successful within, so to speak, its regional hinterland, their inroads into the metropolitan centres of the West have stopped.

As for the larger metropolis—"the East"—they were completely stymied. They were non-existent in the Maritimes. In Ontario, their popular vote declined, and they lost their only seat. But their failure in the metropolitan heartland of the province was even more dramatic. Much was made of vote-splitting between Reform and the Conservatives as a reason for the Liberals' Ontario landslide; but this was hardly the case in the big cities. In Toronto, Reform scarcely exists. In Don Valley, for example, the Liberals polled around 12,000 votes; Reform, less than 2,000. In York Centre, Reform's vote was less than

10 per cent of the Liberals. This sort of result was typical. The same was true in Ottawa, Hamilton (to a lesser extent) and even smaller urban centres. In Thunder Bay, for example, Reform's vote was barely a third of the winning Liberal's total; in Nipissing (which includes North Bay, Mr. Harris's home town) the Liberals polled 20,000 votes, Reform less than 8,000. Reform did somewhat better in Ontario's rural areas, often running second, but their appeal in the larger urban centres can only be described as feeble: reminding us that Reform is *not* a conservative party, but a *hinterland* party, their appeal based on a homogeneous cultural vision, unlikely to find much favour in any modern urban society. In Quebec, the Bloc did rather better; even so, Montreal remains strongly Liberal, and in Quebec City, the Bloc's pluralities were small. In Hull—the third-largest city in the province—the Bloc lost to the Liberals everywhere, and the Liberals carried the rest of the Outaouais, except for a single seat. For both Reform and the Bloc, the popular vote was almost as important as the seat-count: and in both cases, it was stagnant. A good deal of fuss was made about the "magic" figure of 39 per cent, which would allow the Bloc to claim a majority of the francophone vote (they did not quite get it). But this is a pitiful figure; to think that the separatist project could be based on such a narrow section of the population (barely one-half of the linguistic majority, but virtually nobody else) is extraordinary—and is one more reason why partition would be inevitable. For Reform, their vote also failed to increase in the country as a whole and, significantly, declined in Ontario. In both cases, we can see a kind of "high-water" mark. In the western hinterland, there are really no more seats for Reform to win; and even if they did increase their vote in western metropolitan

areas, it wouldn't significantly alter their position. They have reached a stasis. All they can do, *as a hinterland party*, is decline. To increase their vote, especially in Ontario, they would have to fundamentally redefine themselves, which is probably impossible as long as Mr. Manning remains leader—and, of course, such a redefinition would risk losing their hinterland support. Their problem is easy enough to see simply by looking at the Tories. The Tories wish to be a conservative party, but a *national* conservative party—and in fact they are. But this compels them to take a positive position on Quebec, clearly impossible for Reform. The Bloc's situation is rather better. They are a hinterland party, but the hinterland and the metropolis do have one crucial common factor—the French language. This might be enough of a bridge to allow them to conquer *la métropole* and "win"—but it could only ever be a Pyrrhic victory.

This analysis, as everyone—including Mr. Krauthammer— understands, places Ontario at the centre of the situation. But it's easy to overlook the *particular* importance of the Ontario vote. In a general way, Mr. Krauthammer is surely right when he calls Ontario *bland, reasonable, accommodating*—as someone born and bred in the province, I must simply sigh and concede; but, in terms of this election, Mr. Manning, and even M. Charest, might find *brutal, decisive* and *intolerant* more appropriate adjectives, given the vote their parties received.

But however you describe the Ontario vote, there's one word you *can't* use; and that is *regional*. A foreigner, like Mr. Krauthammer, will naturally see the preponderance of Liberal seats in Ontario as equivalent to the Reform sweep in the West;

and Mr. Manning will try, as it were, to bring the Liberals down to his own level by claiming that they are now "just another" regional party. But this completely misreads the Ontario result. Of course—as always—some local factors were at work. After a year or so of Mike Harris, the population was growing leery of "cuts"—as the election began, Mr. Harris occupied second place in all the provincial polls; and Reform and the Conservatives, both associated with Mr. Harris, suffered because of him.

But the very scale of the Liberal victory points to a completely different explanation of what happened in Ontario.

To the extent that Ontario has ever been a "regional" force, its regionalism has always been defined by two words: English and Protestant—as opposed to French and Catholic; as opposed to Quebec. This definition, this opposition, is as old as the rivalry between the Leafs and the Canadiens, and its traditional beneficiaries within Ontario have been the Tories, not the Liberals. It was this older definition of the province that Mr. Manning appealed to in the last days of the campaign, when he attacked the "Quebec" leaders with such ferocity. And what is remarkable about this vote is how massively, how totally, this appeal was rejected.

Indeed, the vote in Ontario was the antithesis of the regional; all considerations, save national considerations, were swept aside as Ontario voted *en bloc* for the only party which, however feebly, could represent the "nation." And the consequences of this are profoundly important. The Ontario vote means that the ruling party, forming the Canadian government, stands on two legs: a substantial group of MPs from Quebec, an even larger group from Ontario. The Ontario vote—however M. Parizeau and the separatists may describe it—means that Quebec is not isolated. The *only* parties that won seats in *English* Ontario were led by men born in *la belle province.*

Mr. Manning, naturally, will object that the definition of the "nation" which Ontario voted to support is, in effect, a regional one—Upper and Lower Canada united again. But this won't do. However one may criticize that old conception of the country, it is a Canada which assumes Quebec, a traditionally valid assumption, and Mr. Manning does not. When Mr. Manning gives a political speech, the Canadian flag—with its red maple leaf—is always prominently displayed behind him, and he will refer to "our common objective of keeping Quebec in the federation." But, as with the rest of his vision—the particular promise that his hinterland politics offers—we are out of time; the flag behind him should be the Union Jack, or the old Red Ensign that flew in Canada during his childhood. For Mr. Manning not only rejects "distinct society," he rejects official bilingualism, and offers Quebec nothing but "a bundle of rights"—which is hard to distinguish from the BNA Act.

Ontario—perhaps just because of its particular anti-French, anti-Quebec history—understood that Reform's conception of Canada leaves Quebec out, *driven* out by Mr. Manning, rather than *led* out by Yves Duceppe; but *out* just the same. Ontario neither wants nor needs this: it has now outgrown a conception of itself, and the country, which sees "the French" as a threat. Ontario, simply because it is a complex, urban, culturally diverse community, understands that no modern definition of society can embrace the narrow, homogeneous vision of Reform. To the extent that any "regional" definition of Ontario was at work in this election, you find it there. And Ontarians, with little difficulty, understand that a vision too narrow for their own province can scarcely govern the country as a whole. In Mr. Manning, the people of Ontario saw a dreadful, looming *national* disaster; and almost in a panic swung behind the Liberals, the only alternative our politics seemed to offer.

Does this mean, then, that the centre of the country has also rejected *promise*?

Hardly.

The particular aspect of *promise* represented by hinterland politics has, for the most obvious reasons, never appealed to Ontario: it is, after all, the metropolis. It is even possible to argue—the separatists probably would—that the nation Ontario voted for is a kind of ideal, only a promise itself. Moreover, the other aspects of *promise* particularly relevant to Ontario—especially the fragmentation of the electorate—are alive and well, only set aside under these very special circumstances.

And here we can see that the future of *promise* is very much alive.

On the weekend before the election, a little secret that will be at the heart of our politics in the next several years was revealed—in *Barron's*, the American financial weekly; and there probably couldn't have been a better place. Canadians love to complain that they're ignored by the American media; but not in *Barron's*. The weekly sister to *The Wall Street Journal*, it is one of the finest financial publications in the world—one of the world's best newspapers, period—and its journalists are well aware of Canada's particular importance as America's most important colony. They keep close tabs on our doings, and are usually a step ahead of most of us. *Oh Boy, Canada!* the title to this article proclaimed . . . and the story below *told us what great financial shape we were in*. That's right—no kidding—and remember, this is a voice from America's capitalist heart, not the NDP newsletter.

"When Canadians go to the polls today," wrote *Barron's*, "they won't be bogged down by thoughts of a nation in fiscal crisis. Instead, for the first time in nearly three decades, they will be able to ponder how the government should spend a budget surplus, which should show up in Canada's coffers as early as next year." This, in a sense, wasn't quite true—that is, Canadians, as they went to the polls, didn't feel this way, since the Liberals had so bungled their campaign. But let me continue with the happy news, just so you'll be prepared:

> Officially, Canada's federal government is expected to run a deficit of $17 billion in the fiscal year ending March 1998. But it will almost surely do better than that. According to Jeffrey Rubin, chief economist at CIBC Wood Gundy Securities in Toronto, Canadian finance minister Paul Martin has overstated the deficit between $6 billion and $8 billion in each of the past three years. "The deficit no longer exists," asserts Rubin. "Given the fiscal framework now in place, next year we're going to see the first federal surplus since 1969. We're now in the 'virtuous circle' of ever-better fiscal results."
>
> . . . Rubin argues that Canada's coming budget surpluses will be large enough to allow for both a substantial tax cut and increased spending in line with inflation and population growth—if Canada forgoes debt repayment. But Rubin considers paying down the debt superfluous. Over the next five years, fairly normal growth alone should drive Canada's debt

Promises, Promises

206

down from 74% of annual economic output to a much more manageable 59%. What's more, a tax cut of $8 billion would increase Canada's economic growth by about 0.75% and create 100,000 new jobs.

"We almost have to have a tax cut," argues Rubin. "The government's looking at a potential $16 billion annual surplus by 2002, and there's no way they'll devote all that to paying down the debt. So, without a tax cut, we're looking at huge new rounds of government spending. That money would be better spent by ordinary taxpayers."[3]

So Jean Charest, it turns out, was right, after all; as Paul Martin will shortly announce, his numbers *did* add up. And no doubt we will get a tax cut, though probably not as large as Mr. Rubin thinks. He underestimates Chaviva Hosek—I never do.

$16 billion! *A year . . .*

Think of it!

Discreetly, even as I write this, friends of Elinor Caplan will be forming consulting firms to advise how this treasure can be spent.

Benefits!

Credits!

Allowances!

Programs, programs, programs!

Think of the *centres* alone—for seniors, the victims of rape and battering, youth, the handicapped and day-care, of course—they will rival banks upon our street corners. And children . . . ah, we will hear so much of them. Poor children. Abused children. Native children. The children of single moms. So many, many children, each deserving of a program: already, they're adding counters in the post offices to hold the application forms. My God—there'll be so much cash, even the artists might get a little . . .

And what of the provincial premiers? Clark, Romanow, Filmon—the whole crew, even Bouchard—will be pacing up and down, full of anxious anticipation. *We want as much as Quebec.* "I think there's a general consensus among the premiers that the devolution of power . . ." Can't you hear their voices, so sincere at the out-thrust microphone? Can't you write the editorials yourself? In the rest of the world, *efficiency* implies economies of scale—in Canada, all problems must be tackled with eleven skyscrapers, minimum, stuffed with our own, uniquely sensitive, *local* bureaucrats. In the rest of the world, *globalization* implies integration, the breaking down of barriers, common currencies—in Canada, an endless division, file cabinets filled with treaties between ourselves. The machinery that runs this side of *promise* has been idling; now it will be put back into gear. The editorial board of *The Toronto Star* stands ready, Michele Landsberg's heart thumps with righteousness, and Peter Mansbridge patiently waits for his cue—to cock his head slightly, then gravely lower his voice as he introduces tonight's carefully scripted atrocity.

Of course, to write like this is to risk the charge of cynicism. In fact, I'm not. Canada does face enormous problems; there's plenty to spend our money on. Indeed, we might well spend some of it on our children—so they can complete their schooling, for example, without bankrupting themselves. But these "problems" and "solutions" will be defined by *promise*, and will, of course, produce endless individual promises. And *promise*, as it has done in the past, will divide us, not bring us together.

Forgoing ideology and history, eschewing analysis and program-matic logic, rooted in irrational conceptions of identity, infan-tile emotions and a vague moralizing vision, the discourse of promise divides us from each other—and, increasingly, within ourselves. Accordingly, the political landscape becomes more and more unreal. One year, the United Nations will declare us the most decent society on the planet—the next, with a little *poof*, we will disappear.

Somewhere, we understand this. And it frightens us. But we have no idea what to do. The extremes of our politics are defined by two hinterland parties pursuing visions that are defined by separatism and exclusion; new covenants which promise to reduce complex, difficult wholes into narrower, simpler parts; to find the future by retreating into golden, mythologized pasts. And the centre, suddenly enriched, can only offer promises which represent the certainty of well-established failure.

We know all this, but what can we do? In frustration, thrash-ing about, we work ourselves deeper and deeper into the swamp, and no one can be optimistic about our chances of emerging. *Promise* has no obvious alternatives; it fears no ideological foes. Everybody loves it—from Preston Manning to Lucien Bouchard, from Jean Charest to Alexa McDonough. To the stock-in-trade of liberals, partially created by the moralistic left, *promise* happily swims with the neo-conservative tide, for it constitutes a radical privatisation of public debate and thought. If there's any hope at all, it comes only from this simple, obvious fact: *promise* doesn't work. It has led us into a terrible crisis, and—here's the little hope—crises can be resolved. The situation is so extreme that we may have to face it. But that is a faint hope, surely. The centre holds—for now, but how much longer? The prime minister muddles along, promising the promises of the past, *the same, only more so*. The leader of the opposition can become prime minister on only one condition—he must bully and frighten Quebec, the oldest settled part of this nation, from Confederation. In the end, of course, this is a democracy; ultimately, only the people can save us from the politicians. And perhaps in the extraordinary, determined vote in Ontario, there's a little sign. But of course it will be a tremendous task. People will have to give up *promise*, that childish heaven, that golden land of childishness, and find a new discourse, a new way of thinking and talking about politics: speaking their two lovely languages, they will have to find a Canadian political speech that allows us to be ourselves but which insists—at last—upon our country.

Endnotes

Chapter One

1   *Webster's New World Dictionary,* Third College Edition, 1076.

2   *The Columbia Encyclopedia,* Fifth Edition, 2226.

3   2 Timothy, 1:1. All Biblical quotations are from the King James Version.

4   *Webster's Dictionary,* 320.

5   Genesis, 17:10.

6   The earliest form of circumcision within Judaism is called the *milah.* It was traditionally done with a flint knife, and only removed the tip of the infant's foreskin. The more radical mutilation (and the most common today) is the *periah.*

7   Exodus, 34:27, 34:28.

8   Exodus, 31:13, 31:16.

9   Robin Lane Fox, *The Unauthorized Version: Truth and Fiction in the Bible* (New York: Knopf, 1992), 124.

10   Galatians, 1:1, 1:12; 1:14; 3:2, 3:5; 3:7; 3:13, 3:14; 3:16; 3:18; 3:19; 3:22; 5:6; 5:14; 4:28.

11   Bronislaw Malinowski, *Magic, Science and Religion and Other Essays* (Westport, Conn.: Greenwood Press, 1984), 88.

12   Ibid., 90.

13   Norman Mailer, *The Armies of the Night* (New York: NAL, 1969), 5.

14 Robert Munsch and Michael Kusugak, *A Promise Is a Promise,* illus. Vladyana Krykorka (Toronto: Annick Press, 1988).

15 Robert Penn Warren, *Promises: Poems 1954–1956* (New York: Random House, 1957), 18.

Chapter Two

1 Peter C. Newman, *Renegade in Power* (Toronto: McClelland & Stewart, 1963), 7. Emphasis added.
2 Ibid., 52.
3 Paul G. Thomas, "The Role of National Party Caucuses," quoted in *The Canadian Political System,* by Richard Van Loon and Michael Wittington, Fourth Edition (Toronto: McGraw-Hill Ryerson, 1987), 334.
4 J.L. Granatstein and J.M. Hitsman, *Broken Promises: A History of Conscription in Canada* (Toronto: Oxford University Press, 1977).
5 Ibid., 142.
6 Newman, *Renegade,* 49.
7 Val Sears, in conversation.

Chapter Three

1 Edward Greenspon and Anthony Wilson-Smith, *Double Vision: The Inside Story of the Liberals in Power* (Toronto: Doubleday, 1996), 138.
2 Lucien Bouchard, *On the Record,* translated by Dominique Clift (Toronto: Stoddart, 1994); *À visage découvert* (Montreal: Boréal, 1992).
   p.3 . . . family; p.3 . . . cult of family; p.5 . . . shrine; p.6 . . .

holy; p.8 . . . *joual*/beautiful language; p.1–2 sometimes even
Chicoutimi [my emphasis]; p.25 . . . Quebec as large city; p.19
. . . our people/isolation; p.2 . . . acting simple; p.18 . . . pride   *Endnotes*
of Saguenay; p.18–19 pride *les Anglais*; p.19 . . . Curiously
enough/vindictiveness; p.36 . . . Irish to the bone [also see the
previous paragraph]; p.36 . . . *his own people* [my emphasis];
p.36 . . . Mulroney set about learning; p.37 . . . Bouchard
paralysed with shame [my emphasis]; p.32 . . . large contingent
of anglophones; p.29 . . . one last time for Duplessis; p.275 . . .
Quebec of old stock/ethnic communities.

3   Most of this data is from an Indian and Northern Affairs
Canada pamphlet, "Comparison of Social Conditions of Registered Indians to the General Population" (Ottawa: July
1995). A fuller picture can be obtained from *Highlights of Aboriginal Conditions, 1991, 1986, Demographic, Social and Economic Characteristics*, Department of Indian and Northern
Affairs (Ottawa: October 1995).

4   *Drumbeat: Anger and Renewal in Indian Country*, edited by
Boyce Richardson (Toronto: Summerhill Press, 1989).

5   Harold Cardinal, *The Unjust Society: The Tragedy of Canada's
Indians* (Edmonton: Hurtig, 1969), 37–38.

6   *Drumbeat*, 8.

7   *Drumbeat*, 3.

8   *Statement of the Government of Canada on Indian Policy, 1969*
(Ottawa: 1969), 5.

9   Ibid., 5.

10 Cardinal, *Unjust Society*, 1.

11 J. Rick Ponting and Roger Gibbons, *Out of Irrelevance: A
Socio-political Introduction to Indian Affairs in Canada* (Toronto:
Butterworths, 1980), 181.

12 Richard Van Loon and Michael Wittington, *The Canadian Political System* (Toronto: McGraw-Hill Ryerson, 1987), 572.

Endnotes 13 Ponting and Gibbons, *Out of Irrelevance,* 27–28. The italics are mine.

Chapter Four

1 *Maclean's,* September 2, 1996.

2 *The Financial Post,* March 22, 1997.

3 *International Herald Tribune,* April 19–20, 1997.

4 Desmond Morton and Glenn Wright, *Winning the Second Battle: Canadian Veterans and the Return to Civilian Life* (Toronto: University of Toronto Press, 1987), 156.

5 Ibid., 57.

6 Ibid., 68.

7 Ibid., 47.

8 Ibid., 73.

9 Ibid., 177.

10 Joseph Schull, *Veneration for Valour: An Assessment of the Veterans Charter* (Ottawa: Information Canada, 1973), 34–35.

11 Ibid., 84. The minister at the time was J.E. Dubé.

12 From an editorial in *The Legion,* April 1990, 2.

13 *The Legion* ("Between Ourselves"), May 1990, 4.

14 *The Legion* ("Between Ourselves"), September 1990, 4–5.

15 Statistics Canada, *The Labour Force,* November 1996 (Table 5).

16 *Strategy for Change,* 23. (This and subsequent references are to a draft, kindly given me by Ms. Doherty-Delorme in the spring of 1997.)

17 Ibid., 3.

18   Ibid., 1.

19   Ibid., 2.

Chapter Five

1   *Maclean's,* June 19, 1995, 10.

2   Rather than detailing each reference in the foregoing, I refer the interested reader to two stories in *Maclean's,* by E. Kaye Fulton—the first on May 6, 1996, the second on May 13. The *Globe's* editorial on Sheila Copps ran on May 2.

3   Scott Feschuk, "CBC counters Liberal charge about town-hall questioners," *The Globe and Mail,* December 14, 1996.

4   "Home Truths About Promises," *Financial Post* editorial, December 13, 1996.

Chapter Six

1   Mark Lisac, *The Klein Revolution* (Edmonton: NeWest Press, 1995), 185.

2   Ibid., 202.

3   Frank Dabbs, *Ralph Klein: A Maverick Life* (Vancouver: Greystone Books, 1995), 103.

4   Ibid., 104 and 105.

5   Bob Rae, *From Protest to Power* (Toronto: Viking, 1996), 280.

Chapter Seven

1   All these quotations are taken from the Web pages maintained by the Reform Party during the 1997 election campaign.

2   John Ralston Saul, *The Doubter's Companion* (Toronto: Viking, 1994), 252.

Endnotes

Chapter Eight

1   E.J. Dionne, "I Like Quebec and Canada, Too," *International Herald Tribune,* June 9, 1997.

2   *International Herald Tribune,* June 7–8, 1997.

3   George Koch, "Oh Boy, Canada!" *Barron's,* June 2, 1997, 24.